The Message of the Book of Revelation

Charles T. Chapman, Jr.

Foreword by
Jerome Kodell, O.S.B.

A Liturgical Press Book

 THE LITURGICAL PRESS
Collegeville, Minnesota

Cover: Remains of the library of Celsus (A.D. 110) in the ancient city of Ephesus.
Photo by Hugh Witzmann, O.S.B. Design by Robin Pierzina, O.S.B.

2	3	4	5	6	7	8	9

Library of Congress Cataloging-in-Publication Data

Chapman, Charles T., 1955-
    The message of the book of Revelation / Charles T. Chapman, Jr. ; foreword by Jerome Kodell.
      p.   cm.
    Includes bibliographical references.
    ISBN 0-8146-2111-2
    1. Bible. N.T. Revelation—Commentaries. I. Title.
BS2825.3.C465 1995
228'.077—dc20   94-16105
                                     CIP

To the memory of Christ's faithful witness,
Charles T. Chapman, Sr. (1920–1988),
and in honor of Betty S. Chapman,
parents whose faithfulness to Christ
will surely win for them the rewards
promised by Christ to those who persevere in faith.

Contents

Foreword

During the spring of 1991, I received a letter from Father Chapman explaining his plan for this commentary on the Book of Revelation and asking permission to spend some time here at our abbey working on it. He was already a friend through his visits here and especially through his excellent work as chaplain to the Episcopal Choir Camp held here for several summers.

I was delighted to hear of his intentions. In spite of great advances in solid biblical knowledge in recent years, the Book of Revelation continues to be a scary riddle for some and a source of wild interpretations and applications for others, above all here in the Bible Belt. Revelation is a beautiful and understandable book, but its true message is still having a hard time getting through. Excellent popular commentaries exist, but none recently has had the space to explain the book phrase by phrase.

Besides that, Father Chapman's pastoral bent and experience gave me confidence that he would be able to judge and select from the wealth of his scholarly studies in order to communicate clearly and directly to the nonspecialist reader. The need for this kind of expertise has come home to me again and again in my experience with study groups using Little Rock Scripture Study.

Father Chapman and I had many discussions as he was developing the commentary; we each learned from one another. As I became convinced of the wider appeal of his book beyond the Episcopal Church, I encouraged him to seek a Roman Catholic publisher and helped him expand his examples for the sake of a Catholic audience. I heartily endorse his commentary.

Abbot Jerome Kodell, O.S.B.
Subiaco Abbey
Subiaco, Arkansas

Preface

The winds of Desert Storm stirred up a number of books on biblical prophecy linking the rise of Saddam Hussein and the prophecies in the Bible concerning ancient Babylon. Preachers linked the Bully of Baghdad with the Whore of Babylon of the Book of Revelation, and openly wondered whether the prophecies of the Apocalypse were finally beginning to come true.

I was perturbed, for, having studied Revelation both in college and in seminary, I believed that it was being misused and misinterpreted by these modern day voices of impending doom. These writers and preachers were working under the assumption that the message of Revelation was unknown to its author and its original readers, hidden under a layer of symbolism which would only become understandable when the events it predicted began to unfold. Instead, I accept the presuppositions of modern scholars that the writer of Revelation did know what message he was communicating through his symbols, and that his readers knew as well, because they were images familiar to them from Jewish apocalyptic literature, both in the Bible and extra-canonical.

The words of my seminary professor who taught the Book of Revelation came back to me: the scholars simply had not presented their findings in a popular way, the way fundamentalists had popularized their interpretations. I determined to try to do just that. Using two of the standard commentaries as my basis and a host of other commentaries and resources (listed in the Bibliography), I undertook to write a phrase-by-phrase interpretation of Revelation for the non-scholarly

reader. Because I focused on this audience, I avoided listing
optional interpretations for the symbols, which would be tire-
some and would not contribute towards an overall picture of
the message of Revelation. Instead, I chose the most reasonable and consistent interpretations and described them as
clearly as possible. I saved the words "probably" or "likely"
only for the more obscure symbols, desiring to convey the idea
that more is known about Revelation than not.

I want to acknowledge with gratitude the Episcopal Dio-
cese of Kansas and the parish of Grace Episcopal Church, Win-
field, Kansas, for the continuing education grants and time off
I received from them for the writing of this book. I also wish
to thank the community of Subiaco Abbey, Subiaco, Arkansas,
where this book was written, and Abbot Jerome Kodell for his
valuable suggestions and support of this project.

It is my sincere hope that this commentary will assist those
who are mystified by the Book of Revelation, and show that
its message is truly one of hope and glory in the lordship of
Christ over history and the ways of humankind.

The Rev. Charles T. Chapman, Jr.
Amarillo, Texas
August 18, 1992

Finding a Place to Begin

Many books of the Bible can be read, enjoyed, and reasonably understood by people with little background in biblical studies. Of course, the more Bible study the reader has had, the more the reader will understand. Even if a person knows little about being a shepherd, for example, there is still great meaning in the words, "The Lord is my shepherd, I shall not want."

Not so with the Book of Revelation. The average reader looks at Revelation and sees a great, confusing jumble of symbols and images which appear to make no sense whatsoever. Yet, so much is known about the book and its contents, things about which we can be reasonably sure regarding the overall message of the book (if not the meaning of specific images), that it should not be a mystery.

The task of deciphering Revelation's images is not made any easier by widespread traditions about the book which see it as a forecast of the end of the world. Perhaps you are asking, "Well, isn't it?" While a simple "yes" or "no" would answer that question, it wouldn't tell the most important part—why.

To start our study of Revelation, we should begin as we do with any other book of the Bible. There are certain questions we should ask, certain things we need to know in order to interpret the book properly. These common-sense questions include:

1. *What kind of literature is the book?* Not all of the books of the Bible are the same type of literature. We find history, short story, parable, drama, poetry, hymns, sermons, tracts, letters, that special kind of biography we call the Gospels, and others.

2. *Who wrote the book, when was it written, and who first received and read it?* Knowing the identity of the author may help us

compare it with other biblical writings, leading to greater understanding. Knowing when a book was written and who first read it can help us understand historical references, identify the purpose for writing, decipher references the author makes to current events, etc.

3. *What was the author's basic message? What was his purpose in writing?* As we read a biblical book we employ the scientific method. Based on our reading we formulate a theory about a book's basic message and purpose. Further study leads us to modify or confirm our theory, and helps explain difficult passages.

Perhaps it would be helpful if we applied these basic questions to a book which is much less difficult to understand, about which much more is known for certain. Here are answers to the above three questions as applied to the Book of Galatians:

1. *Form of Literature:* Galatians isn't really a book, but a long letter. It follows the standard outline of a letter as used in those days, with one exception which has to do with the author's mood when he wrote it. Knowing what the standard outline of a letter was in those days, as well as comparing this to other letters St. Paul wrote, helps us to know that the author left out a section usually included in a letter.

2. *Author, Date, and Original Recipients:* St. Paul wrote the letter to the Christians in the churches in the region of Galatia, meaning either the Roman province of Galatia or, more likely, what we would call northern Turkey. He wrote it in the mid to late 50s A.D., at a time when a group of Jewish Christians called by scholars "Judaizers" were trying to force the new Gentile Christians into practicing Jewish rituals and laws.

3. *Purpose and Central Message:* St. Paul's basic message to the Galatians is that in Christ they have been set free from the need to earn their salvation by obeying a set of laws. However, he takes the opportunity to warn them not to use this freedom as an excuse to behave in any way they please.

In this example of the Letter to the Galatians we see that it would be very important to investigate, read between the lines, and learn as much as possible about the Judaizers, because this letter was written mainly in response to their teachings and claims. To ignore this information would be to ignore the very reason why the book was written.

It is the same with Revelation. We must ask these same three basic questions, reading between the lines in order to try to discover the purpose and message of the author of this mystifying book. Only then can we find that the door leading to understanding is not permanently locked after all; and only then can we begin to learn the keys to opening the door of understanding.

A. What Kind of Literature Is the Book?

This question is perhaps the most important to answer first for Revelation, because it holds the biggest key to discovering the answers to the other two questions. How do we go about identifying the type of literature of Revelation? We must assume the role of a Sherlock Holmes by identifying clues, lining up and questioning suspects, and seeing what we get when we piece it all together.

CLUE NUMBER 1: *A Prophecy*

What clues are found in Revelation that will help us identify its type of literature? One of the first clues, found in 1:3, is that the writer calls this book a prophecy. This immediately brings up a problem. Most people think of a prophecy as some kind of prediction or forecast of the future. Although that is what the word means now, it isn't necessarily what the word meant in biblical times. A prophecy, as someone once put it, is not a fore-telling, but a forth-telling. In other words, in a prophecy the speaker is telling forth the thoughts of God as the speaker has been led by the Holy Spirit to know them. Prophecy is not really forecasting the future. The classic pattern of an Old Testament prophecy is this: ''Thus says the Lord. In the past I freed you from slavery in Egypt and led you into this land, as I promised I would. Here I made of you a great nation. However, now you are being unfaithful (here the speaker would list the ways in which they are being unfaithful). Therefore, if you continue in your unfaithfulness, this is what I am going to do (here the speaker tells God's intentions). However, if you repent and return unto me, I will protect you and you will be great like your ancestors.''

Notice how the emphasis is on the present, on the times and events of the speaker. The part we usually think of as a forecast is not a prediction at all. It is a conditional statement of what God intends to do, with Israel's choice being the determining factor.

So also Revelation: The emphasis in the book is on the situation of the writer and of his readers. The writer describes for his original readers their situation from God's perspective, and then announces what God intends to do about it. He proclaims the rewards of those who are faithful and endure, and he proclaims God's warnings and intentions to destroy the wicked.

CLUE NUMBER 2:
Beasties and Ghosties and Things That Go Bump in the Night!

A second clue about the type of literature of Revelation is the veritable zoo of fantastic creatures that populate its pages, including a seven-headed beast with ten horns, six-winged seraphs covered all over with eyes, and a prostitute riding on a monster—all of these add confusion and frustration to the casual reader. Yet, these are symbols which tell the message of the book in coded form, understood by the writer and the people to whom he first sent the book, but not by outsiders.

How are we ever to discover what these beasties symbolize? Few persons take them literally; most believe them to be symbolic. However, the agreement ends here because so many writers differ about the meaning of these symbols. Help comes to us in the fact that there are other writings like Revelation, and some of them are in the Bible.

For two or three hundred years before the birth of Christ, many Jews were giving up on the hope which the prophets had proclaimed. They no longer expected that God was going to restore his people to full and free nationhood and, through them, reform the entire world. This prophetic vision was dying because of the repeated invasions and enslavements of the Jews by foreign powers: the Greeks, the Egyptians, the Syrians, and the Romans. So, they began to write books expressing a new idea. The new books declared that God was not going to restore Israel and reform this world; rather, they said that God is going to destroy the wicked of this world and create a new heaven and earth with the few righteous people who are left (as Genesis tells us God did in Noah's day). In order to give their books the appearance of ancient wisdom from the past, and to give them authority, they wrote under the names of people such as Enoch, Moses, and other famous and influential men of old. (While we would not stand for it if a modern writer were to claim that some famous person from the past had written his work, they did such things back then when they believed it served the truth and its proclamation. As we will see in our study of Revelation, we must beware of applying our standards to practices and expressions of former days.)

These writers claimed to be revealing God's hidden plan for the world. For this reason their writings have come to be known as "apocalyptic literature." The word *apocalyptic* comes from the Greek word *apocalypsis* which means "something uncovered which was previously hidden; a revelation." Sections of Ezekiel, Daniel, Joel, and Isaiah are apocalyptic.

The first word of Revelation is *apocalypsis*. Indeed, in some Bibles the Book of Revelation is called "The Apocalypse." The book begins this way because the author wants to communicate to his readers a message which he has received from God and which was previously hidden. It is also a clue to us that he is writing in the tradition of the apocalyptic writers. Indeed, an investigation of the symbols and themes in apocalyptic writings and in Revelation reveals a high degree of similarity; so much so, that we can often interpret symbols in Revelation because they are directly borrowed from the older works whose meaning is fairly well known.

Some writers have said that the Book of Daniel contains the key to understanding Revelation. They are correct if they are referring to the fact that so many of the symbols used in the two books are similar. However, similar symbols can have different applications in different times. So, we must beware of trying to interpret Daniel and Revelation as if they were referring to the same future events simply because their symbols are similar. They deal with separate events in their own respective time periods using a common vocabulary of symbolism.

We must also keep in mind that apocalyptic writers wrote their books as if they had been written many years before their time. They often described things happening in their own time as if they were a vision of the future. Again, we would not stand for it if a writer in a newspaper in July of 1994 were to write: ''And in those days a President shall arise who shall make war on ancient Babylon [Iraq], and who shall nominate a son of Africa [Judge Thomas] to the highest tribunal of the land [the Supreme Court],'' and then try to make us think it had been written hundreds of years earlier. Writers of apocalyptic literature did this because they believed they had a significant revelation from God, and they wanted to present their revelation in all its power and importance.

It should be said at this point that the original Jewish-Christian readers of Revelation were familiar with the symbolism used in the book and would have been able to explain it to their Gentile brothers and sisters in the churches. Because the percentage of Jewish Christians shrank so rapidly after the faith was opened up to the Gentiles, the original meaning of these apocalyptic symbols was lost. Now, however, armed with the tools of modern studies in apocalyptic literature, we can find help to ''decode'' the message of Revelation.

This leads to another question: Why would the author wish to encode his message in this secret system of symbols? He did this both to dramatize his message and to hide it from the enemies of the community who are described in the book. In Revelation John is writing about the Romans. If he had said plainly that the Roman emperor got his power from Satan, the Romans would have severely treated anyone caught with a copy of the book, if indeed they had allowed him to send it to the churches in the first place. He expresses his message in symbols both to hide the message, and to make it more real, depending upon who is reading the book.

So we have seen how Revelation is both a prophecy and an apocalyptic writing. The author sought to describe God's view of human history and warn humanity where it was going, believing that history was irredeemable, hopelessly corrupt, and would end with a great act of divine intervention. He expressed this message using fantastic imagery common to other ancient apocalyptic writings.

B. Who Wrote the Book, When Was It Written, and Who Were Its First Readers?

Questions concerning the author, date, and first recipients of Revelation seem easy compared to the task of deciphering the book's symbols. However, the question of authorship in particular is rather tricky. In 1:1, 4, and 9 the author identifies himself as John. The question is, which John? The John whom most people immediately think of, the one tradition says wrote the book, is St. John the Apostle. However, the traditional title of the book is not "The Revelation of St. John the Apostle," but "St. John the Divine." "Divine" means "seer," that is, one who is granted a vision of the future. (Irrelevant but interesting to note is that the largest Gothic church in the world, still unfinished at this writing, is the Cathedral of St. John the Divine in New York.)

The primary reason for doubting the authorship of John the Apostle is that, as we have mentioned earlier, the writers of apocalyptic writings usually used pseudonyms—pen names—when they wrote. This leads scholars to wonder whether Revelation was written by someone using the name of John the Apostle in order to ride the coattails of his authority as an apostle. Other possibilities include: the author was one of the disciples of John the Apostle and, since he learned what he knew about the faith from the apostle, he named his Apocalypse for him; or, Revelation was written by John the Elder, a student of the Beloved Disciple (the author of John's Gospel, even though he himself was not John) who appears to have written 2 and 3 John. Any other discussion of the identity of the author of Revelation is only so much educated guesswork. Suffice it to say that the writer is closely associated with the same group of people that gave us the Gospel of John and the Letters of John and had their headquarters in Ephesus. We will go ahead and call the author of Revelation "John" even though there is much uncertainty about who he was.

John made extensive use of the Old Testament in describing his message. It must be emphasized that in the Book of Revelation, although the writer wishes us to understand that he is communicating a new revelation from God, his revelation is not inconsistent with what was previously revealed in Scripture. Rather, John took images from the Old Testament which spoke of circumstances similar to those of him and his readers, images familiar to them, and recast them in order to apply their eternal truth to his day. Our task is to see that, just as John did not consider Zechariah, Daniel, or Ezekiel to be merely tracts for their own time with no relevance for his own, we must see Revelation as more than a tract for John's time. It may not be a blueprint of late twentieth-century history, but it is not a time-locked irrelevancy either.

As far as the original readership and the date Revelation was written goes, more is known. The recipients of the book were the Christians of Asia Minor, the Roman province we now know as Turkey. The first section of Revelation consists of seven letters to churches in this province. As these churches are representative of all the churches in Asia Minor, so this letter contains a message for all Christians of their day, and ours.

As we identify current events behind the symbolic language of Revelation, we discover that it was most likely written at the time of the emperor Domitian's persecutions against the Christians, around the mid-90s A.D. This leads us to summarize and make the following points:

1. The readers of Revelation understood the message John was writing to them. If we accept the idea that the book was written and sent during a time of persecution, then we can agree that it is highly unlikely that John would have sent those afflicted Christians a message of comfort which they could not understand.

2. Based on the nature of biblical prophecy, we understand that Revelation is describing events occurring basically during the lifetime of its readers, as well as anticipating the plans of God for their near future. This is supported by the prologue

which says that the things described in the book "must happen soon" (1:1), and that "the appointed time is near" (1:3). This is in contrast to the Book of Daniel, where Daniel is told that his vision will be fulfilled only after many days (Dan 8:26).

3. Therefore, as we look for actual events in history as explanations for what is described in Revelation, we should not be looking at events in the second half of the twentieth century, as Hal Lindsey in *The Late Great Planet Earth* and other writers have done. Rather, we should be looking at events in the second half of the first century A.D. in the Roman Empire.

C. What Was the Author's Basic Message? What Was His Purpose in Writing?

With this background, we can now turn to Revelation and see what message John wrote to the churches, and think about what Revelation is saying to us today. We can summarize the message of Revelation in this way: John describes history as a cycle of nationalism, war, famine, and death. God warns the Roman emperor, who has declared himself to be a god and is persecuting the Church like a new Nero, that the empire will be destroyed if he does not repent. Various natural disasters underscore the warning. Next, John describes the story of salvation as a cosmic battle between good and evil, with the person of Jesus Christ at its center. John then describes the destruction of Rome, the return of Christ as a victorious warrior, the era of peace which Christ establishes, the destruction of the old universe, and the creation of a new universe in which God lives in a new Jerusalem on a new planet Earth inhabited by all the blessed of God (the wicked, along with death and hell, having been tossed into a lake of fire). He closes the message by urging his readers to pray that Christ will soon return.

A word about the arrangement and structure of the book: Four sections of the book, those concerning the letters, seals, trumpets, and bowls of wrath, clearly contain seven sections. Attempts have been made to show that the book has an outline of a prologue, seven parts each with seven sections, and an epilogue. Although it would be wonderful if the text of Revelation supported this arrangement, it does not.

Things to note:

1. John does not follow a linear progression of events. That is, he does not describe events one by one in the order in which they occur, as if he were reading a time line. Rather, to build a sense of anticipation, he jumps back and forth and describes again an event which he has already described before. One of the confusing things about this is that some interpreters fail to take notice of the fact that he is retelling an event, so that they try to make the retelling out to be a second, different event.

2. Setting is very important in Revelation. John as narrator moves back and forth between heaven and earth. To call attention to this we will, at times, mark the change of John's location with a separate line labelled "Setting."

3. Revelation cannot simply be a tract for its time—it contains truth which applies today as well. At the end of each segment there will be a brief section labelled "Thinking Aloud," consisting of this author's reflections concerning the segment's applicability to our own day and age.

The Book of Revelation

Prologue (1:1-8)

I. Prologue

1 ¹The revelation of Jesus Christ, which God gave to him, to show his servants what must happen soon. He made it known by sending his angel to his servant John, ²who gives witness to the word of God and to the testimony of Jesus Christ by reporting what he saw. ³Blessed is the one who reads aloud and blessed are those who listen to this prophetic message and heed what is written in it, for the appointed time is near.

II. Letters to The Churches of Asia

Greeting ⁴John, to the seven churches in Asia: grace to you and peace from him who is and who was and who is to come, and from the seven spirits before his throne, ⁵and from Jesus Christ, the faithful witness, the firstborn of the dead and ruler of the kings of the earth. To him who loves us and has freed us from our sins by his blood, ⁶who has made us into a kingdom, priests for his God and Father, to him be glory and power forever [and ever]. Amen.

⁷ Behold, he is coming amid the clouds,
and every eye will see him,
even those who pierced him.
All the peoples of the earth will lament him.
Yes. Amen.

⁸"I am the Alpha and the Omega," says the Lord God, "the one who is and who was and who is to come, the almighty."

1:1 "The revelation of Jesus Christ, which God gave to him": It is extremely important to note from the very beginning the correct name of this book, in order to ensure that it is properly interpreted and used. Taken from its first line, its name is NOT "The Book of Revelations," as if this were a series of separate, individual revelations which may be separated and interpreted apart from one another according to the reader's best imagination. Rather, this is one revelation, a unity, a whole, which must be interpreted as a whole.

Further, it is essential to understand that this is not a completely new revelation in the sense that everything revealed herein was unknown before. The message of the Book of Revelation follows strongly in the tradition of Isaiah, Jeremiah, Ezekiel, Daniel, and Zechariah, as we will see by the extensive references in Revelation to these and other Old Testament books. What was new was John's application of these Old Testament prophetic statements to his own situation in 95 A.D.

Since John sent his book from Patmos to Asia Minor, it begins in the same way a letter did in those days. John tells how the revelation he records was first given to Christ by God, who alone knows "the times or seasons that the Father has established by his own authority" (Acts 1:7).

"what must happen soon": Here and in verse 3 ("the appointed time is near") we are reminded that John fully expected everything in his Revelation to happen soon after he wrote and sent his message. This underscores the idea that we should not interpret Revelation as a prediction of late twentieth-century events.

1:3 "Blessed is the one who reads aloud . . . this prophetic message": This refers to the lector who will read Revelation to the seven Churches to which it is addressed, and is reminiscent of a bishop's blessing of a deacon prior to the reading of the gospel at Mass.

1:4-7 These verses summarize the hopeful and encouraging message of the entire book.

1:4 "the seven spirits before his [God's] throne": This refers to the sevenfold Spirit of God given to the Messiah in Isaiah 11:1-2. It also refers to Zechariah 4:6 where God's message is, "Not by an army, nor by might, but by my spirit, says the LORD of hosts. . . ." This is an example of how John uses brief references to the Old Testament in order to say much in a few words. He reassures the persecuted Christians to whom he is writing that they need not fear their own weakness, for the strength of God's Spirit is within them.

THINKING ALOUD

How often do we hesitate in something we might do for the advance of God's kingdom because we fear our own weakness? How often, when proposing ways to overcome difficulties in the ministry and mission of the Church do we hear primarily a chorus of reasons why the enterprise will not work? We must depend not on our own strength, power, cleverness, or might, but on the working of the Holy Spirit of God who dwells within each of us through our baptism. It is faithfulness, not ability, that God requires from us. And where we are faithful, God supplies the gifts, the ability to accomplish that to which God calls us.

1:5 "the firstborn of the dead and ruler of the kings of the earth": Notice Psalm 89:28 about the Messiah: "I myself make him firstborn, / Most High over the kings of the earth."

"by his blood": That is, by his obedient death on the cross. The Hebrews believed that the life force of a living creature resides in the creature's blood (note Lev 17:11). Therefore, "to shed blood" and "by means of his blood" meant in their minds, "to take a life" and "by means of his giving of his life," respectively.

1:6 John symbolizes the Church as a new Israel, and uses Old Testament statements about Israel to describe the Church. It is very important to keep this in mind, as in most places in the book whenever Israel is mentioned, it means the Church. It is also important that we do not use this to support a "replacement theology" which suggests that the Jews, having rejected Christ, are no longer covenant people with God. This theology was directly responsible for opening the way to the Holocaust in the minds of the German people. It is appropriate to think of the Church in the same biblical terms as Israel, even to the point of calling the Church "Israel," because both are covenant people of God as expressed in Holy Scripture.

"a kingdom, priests for his God": This recalls Exodus 19:6: "You shall be to me a kingdom of priests." John is reminding his readers of their destiny in Christ, a destiny which need not wait for the arrival of the future in order to be fulfilled.

1:7 This verse recalls Zechariah 12:10b which says, "and they shall look on him whom they have thrust through, and they shall mourn for him as one mourns for an only son." Only the Gospel of John (19:31-37) tells of Jesus' side being pierced at his crucifixion, and it cites this verse in Zechariah as a prophecy of that event. This is significant because the Gospel of John and Revelation are considered to be from the same Christian community. The idea expressed in this verse suggests the kind of turning of the tables which is a major theme in Revelation.

This verse also inspired the Advent hymn-poem by Charles Wesley:

> Lo! He comes with clouds descending, once for our
>   salvation slain . . .
> Those who set at naught and sold him, pierced,
>   and nailed him to the tree,
> Deeply wailing, shall their true Messiah see.

Revelation contains many scenes of heavenly worship and has inspired as much if not more music as any other New Testament book.

THINKING ALOUD

Christ is the faithful witness; he is the trustworthy bearer of the revelation of God, faithfully revealing to us who God is and what God is like both in his words and in his life as portrayed in the Gospels.

Christ did not achieve his status in any easy fashion, nor did he show us his love by buying us a dozen roses. It was by his obedient, sacrificial death. The Christian life is the call to respond to this sacrificial love.

John is asserting the belief which is the foundation of his faith that all is not lost for his persecuted community. Christ is yet to appear once and for all time to inherit the world as kingdom of God.

1:8 John introduces Christ, champion of the persecuted Church, and completes his summary of the book's content in his description of the vision which follows.

"the Alpha and the Omega": These are first and last letters of the Greek alphabet, used to declare that God is the Eternal One, in whom is the beginning and ending of all things.

Section 1: The Seven Letters

A. Introduction to the Seven Letters

The First Vision ⁹I, John, your brother, who share with you the distress, the kingdom, and the endurance we have in Jesus, found myself on the island called Patmos because I proclaimed God's word and gave testimony to Jesus. ¹⁰I was caught up in spirit on the Lord's day and heard behind me a voice as loud as a trumpet, ¹¹which said, "Write on a scroll what you see and send it to the seven churches: to Ephesus, Smyrna, Pergamum, Thyatira, Sardis, Philadelphia, and Laodicea." ¹²Then I turned to see whose voice it was that spoke to me, and when I turned, I saw seven gold lampstands ¹³and in the midst of the lampstands one like a son of man, wearing an ankle-length robe, with a gold sash around his chest. ¹⁴The hair of his head was as white as white wool or as snow, and his eyes were like a fiery flame. ¹⁵His feet were like polished brass refined in a furnace, and his voice was like the sound of rushing water. ¹⁶In his right hand he held seven stars. A sharp two-edged sword came out of his mouth, and his face shone like the sun at its brightest.

¹⁷When I caught sight of him, I fell down at his feet as though dead. He touched me with his right hand and said, "Do not be afraid. I am the first and the last, ¹⁸the one who lives. Once I was dead, but now I am alive forever and ever. I hold the keys to death and the netherworld. ¹⁹Write down, therefore, what you have seen, and what is happening, and what will happen afterwards. ²⁰This is the secret meaning of the seven stars you saw in my right hand, and of the seven gold lampstands: the seven stars are the angels of the seven churches, and the seven lampstands are the seven churches.

Setting: John is on the island of Patmos describing a vision while in the Spirit.

1:9-11 In these verses John tells how he came to write this book.

1:9 **"Patmos"**: This was a Roman prison island in the Aegean Sea.

1:10 **"I was caught up in spirit"**: John suggests that he entered some kind of ecstatic state. This also underscores his conviction that his message is from God through the Holy Spirit, in the best tradition of the Old Testament prophets (recall the Nicene Creed, which says that the Spirit spoke through the prophets).

"the Lord's day": Sunday. In all of literature this is the first time Sunday is called "the Lord's Day."

"a voice as loud as a trumpet": In Isaiah 58:1 the prophet is told to "lift up your voice like a trumpet blast." A trumpet was used to warn a city, summon the people, announce the arrival of the king, or introduce a royal proclamation. All of these meanings apply here.

1:11 **"Ephesus, Smyrna, Pergamum, Thyatira, Sardis, Philadelphia, and Laodicea"**: Why these seven churches? Revelation was sent as a circular letter to be read in the churches, and the cities are listed in the order in which the letter would travel when sent from Patmos. Each of these cities was the location of the district post office for their respective regions. The book arrived first at John's home city of Ephesus, which was the most important city politically, commercially, and religiously, in Asia Minor. Ephesus was also home to the Johannine community, the group of Christians that produced the biblical books bearing the name of John.

The number seven also represents completeness, since there are seven days in a week. It is a holy number, since the seventh day is the Sabbath. So, by extension, "seven churches" means "all of God's holy people" as represented by these seven, and not these seven alone.

Some modern authors have suggested that the seven churches represent seven ages in Church history. This option is best put aside, since the letters to the churches clearly indicate that they were written to real, specific churches in actual places in the first century A.D.

1:12 "**seven gold lampstands**": This recalls Zechariah 4:2, mentioned earlier, in which Israel is represented as a golden lampstand with seven lamps. John is going to tell us through the words of Christ that "the seven lampstands are the seven churches" (1:20). Therefore, what we have here is a vision of Christ who is present in power in the midst of his Church on earth.

1:13-16 These verses contain John's first vision of Jesus. It is important to keep in mind that these are "literary visions." That is, John expressed his insight into the truth by using images from Old Testament books (especially apocalyptic ones). John's description of Christ is a composite of the description of God in Ezekiel chapter 1, the vision of the Son of Man in Daniel 7:13, and of an angelic being in Daniel 10:5. Thus, in John's understanding, Jesus is the Holy One sent from God to bring about the kingdom of God on earth.

1:13 "**one like a son of man**": Originally, "son of man" (as used in Numbers 23:19) meant a human person. However, in Daniel 7:13 the writer says that while in a dream (the "visions during the night") he saw "One like a son of man coming, on the clouds of heaven; . . . he reached the Ancient One and was presented before him." Thus, the term "Son of Man" came to mean this divine, cosmic, humanlike personage whom God would send from heaven to establish God's kingdom on earth in its fullness. After the resurrection the disciples realized that Jesus is that Son of Man.

"**a robe that reached down to his feet**": The average working person wouldn't wear a robe such as this—you can't work in it! This is the robe of a very wealthy person who doesn't have to work, like a king.

"**a gold cloth was wrapped around his chest**": Ezekiel reported a shining brightness the color of amber around God's waist, and Daniel's angel in chapter 10 was clothed in linen with gold around his waist. In the ancient world kings wore a golden clasp at their waist, and priests wore a sash around their chest. Jesus/God is a royal priest.

1:14 "**white as wool or snow**": This is drawn from Daniel's description of the Ancient of Days (God); it represents holiness and wisdom. The image of the wool may also call to mind the Johannine name for Christ, the "lamb of God."

"eyes looked like flames of fire": Daniel's angel (ch. 10) had "eyes like flaming torches." This symbolizes piercing insight.

1:15 "feet were glowing like bronze": Elijah's cherubim had bronze feet: represents surefootedness, standing firm.

"voice . . . like the roar of a waterfall": Ezekiel 43:2 says that the sound of the coming of God's glory was like "the roaring of many waters." Christ speaks with the voice of God.

1:16 "seven stars in his right hand": Here is an example of Revelation interpreting itself for us: verse 20 tells us that the seven stars are the angels of the seven churches. To be in Christ's right hand is to be under his authority and protection.

"a sharp double-edged sword was coming from his mouth": Note Hebrews 4:12: "the word of God is living and active, sharper than any two-edged sword . . . able to discern reflections and thoughts of the heart." Isaiah says that the Messiah will strike the earth with the rod of his mouth. This symbolizes Jesus as pronouncing God's judgement. (Cf. the Creed, "He shall come again to judge the living and the dead.")

"His face was shining": The faces of the righteous and of angels are often described as shining with divine radiance.

1:17 "I fell down at his feet as though dead": This is exactly what happened to Daniel when the angelic being spoke to him in Daniel 10:9.

1:18 "the keys of death and the underworld": This means that Jesus was given power over the abode of departed spirits, which refers to the ancient Hebrew belief that the dead went to Sheol to await judgement.

1:20 "the seven stars are the angels": Both the Pleiades and the Big Dipper are made of seven stars. The angels in apocalyptic are always supernatural beings, so these would not be the leaders of the churches, as some have suggested. These are either the guardians of the seven churches (Daniel speaks of guardian angels, such as Michael, guardian of Israel), or in some sense they are angels which represent the churches as they are now, while the lampstands represent the churches as they are meant to become.

Each of these letters contains the following components:

a. A single description of Christ, drawn from the list of descriptions in chapter 1, which is relevant to the specific city addressed;

b. A description of the church's good works;

c. Christ's warning and/or encouragement;

d. Christ's promise to those who overcome, expressed specifically to the church addressed.

THINKING ALOUD

In contrast to earthly forces that seem so numerous, powerful, and bent toward evil, Christ is present in power among his churches. He is not merely the carpenter of Nazareth, although that is who he is; he is the Divine One destined from before time to inherit the kingdom of God. He speaks with words of judgement against the evil forces of the earth. He is the faithful witness, whose life and words truthfully reveal the nature and love of God.

Let this inspire the Church to minister and proclaim the gospel with boldness, confidence, and with no trace of shame or embarrassment.

B. *The Seven Letters*

1. THE LETTER TO EPHESUS (2:1-7)

2 To Ephesus [1]"To the angel of the church in Ephesus, write this:

" 'The one who holds the seven stars in his right hand and walks in the midst of the seven gold lampstands says this: [2]"I know your works, your labor, and your endurance, and that you cannot tolerate the wicked; you have tested those who call themselves apostles but are not, and discovered that they are impostors. [3]Moreover, you have endurance and have suffered for my name, and you have not grown weary. [4]Yet I hold this against you: you have lost the love you had at first. [5]Realize how far you have fallen. Repent, and do the works you did at first. Otherwise, I will come to you and remove your lampstand from its place, unless you repent. [6]But you have this in your favor: you hate the works of the Nicolaitans, which I also hate.

[7]" ' "Whoever has ears ought to hear what the Spirit says to the churches. To the victor I will give the right to eat from the tree of life that is in the garden of God." ' "

a.   **2:1**   Christ is the Lord, holding the churches in his hand, which corresponds to the fact that Ephesus was the chief city in Asia Minor.

Ephesus as a city was first in honor in the Roman province of Asia in society, government, and religion, both pagan and Christian. Recall the refrain at the end of each of the letters: "Hear what the Spirit says to the churches." The church of Ephesus serves as an example to all the other churches.

While Pergamum was the Roman capital of Asia, any new governor had to go through Ephesus out of respect for this city on his way to Pergamum. Ephesus was a major port with a major trade route leading into Asia Minor.

Long before the Greeks came, the Ephesians worshipped the Mother God, whose temple was a wonder of the ancient world. When the Greeks brought their goddess Artemis, the Ephesians simply renamed their mother god "Artemis" and continued as they had before. When the Romans came they built a temple to Julius Caesar, the divine one. Thus Ephesus was a religious center for pagan Asia Minor.

Ephesus was also the chief city for the Church in Asia Minor. Tradition locates the Apostle John there, and the books named for John, including Revelation, emerged from there. Paul spent three years of his ministry there, and the Pastoral Epistles that bear his name were written there.

b.   **2:2-3**   The Ephesian church was an example through their hard work and endurance. Endurance is a major theme of these letters, being the path to ultimate victory.

The Ephesian church was also an example in the way they exposed "those who called themselves apostles." These were people who claimed to belong to that group of apostles who did not belong to the Twelve (e.g., St. Paul). Exposing false teaching is a major theme in all the writings named for John.

c. **2:4-6** As so often occurs, people who have endured much and who have been threatened with false teachers have grown coldhearted and have left the love they had at first. For a church in the tradition and community that produced the Gospel and Letters of John, which focus so much on the love of God and love for one another, this sin of allowing love to grow cold would be an especially grievous and serious one.

John encourages them to think about the love they had at first and to return to it. This is an important message to all those who seek to protect right belief (orthodoxy): in the quest for truth, do not lose sight of the love which first drew us to Christ and to one another. Apparently the Ephesians took this instruction from John to heart, for Ignatius, writing in his long letter to the Ephesians twenty years later, is full of praise for this church which he calls "deservedly happy." He says that they are known for their good deeds and harmonious love, and for living in blameless unity and good discipline.

"The Nicolaitans" are people seeking to lead the church into improper actions. Here the Ephesians are praised for protecting right practice (orthopraxy). The identity of the Nicolaitans is unknown. The word may mean "followers of Nicolas," but Nicolas is also unknown. What is clear is that they are a group involved in activities which John and the Ephesians hate.

d. **2:7** The Ephesian church is also an example of the reward of remaining faithful to Christ. They live in a city (as we saw above) dedicated to Artemis, goddess of fertility and growth, including the fruitfulness and growth of vegetation. Compare this to Christ's promise to the Ephesian Christians that they will be able to "eat from the tree of life in the garden of God." Here the last book in the Bible brings us back to the first, where in Genesis 3:22-23 Adam and Eve, having disobeyed by eating of the tree of knowledge, are expelled from God's garden of Eden lest they eat of the tree of life and live eternally in that fallen state. Thus we come full circle: In Christ fallen humanity is redeemed and readmitted to the garden, there to eat of the fruit once denied them. This tree will be further described in 22:2.

THINKING ALOUD

It does require hard work to be faithful to right believing (orthodoxy) and right practice (orthopraxy). Perhaps our modern toleration comes not from a desire to be more accepting of others, but from laziness.

If the error of those who are too lenient is that they tolerate false belief and practice, the error of those who champion orthodoxy and orthopraxy is that they grow to love doctrine and practice more than they love people, or God.

2. The Letter to Smyrna (2:8-11)

To Smyrna   ⁸"To the angel of the church in Smyrna, write this:

" 'The first and the last, who once died but came to life, says this: ⁹"I know your tribulation and poverty, but you are rich. I know the slander of those who claim to be Jews and are not, but rather are members of the assembly of Satan. ¹⁰Do not be afraid of anything that you are going to suffer. Indeed, the devil will throw some of you into prison, that you may be tested, and you will face an ordeal for ten days. Remain faithful until death, and I will give you the crown of life.

¹¹" ' "Whoever has ears ought to hear what the Spirit says to the churches. The victor shall not be harmed by the second death." '

a.   **2:8**   Christ is the one "who once died but came to life." This relates directly to the city of Smyrna which "died" when it was destroyed six hundred years before Christ, and came to life when it was later rebuilt. Also, Smyrna was the location of a cult dedicated to the god Cybele, who according to mythology died and rose again.

b.   **2:9**   In this verse we see the first sign that not all of the Church's problems came from the Romans. The Jews also persecuted the Christians by throwing them out of the synagogues. The phrase, "those who claim to be Jews but are not," is best interpreted by Romans 9:6b-8, quoted here from the *New Revised Standard Version:* "For not all who are of Israel are

Israel, nor are they all children of Abraham because they are his descendants, but 'It is through Isaac that descendants shall bear your name.' This means that it is not the children of the flesh who are the children of God, but the children of the promise.'' This echoes the words of Jesus in the Gospel of John (and thus shows a consistent picture within the writings that bear the name "John"), "You belong to your father the devil and you willingly carry out your father's desires. He was a murderer from the beginning and does not stand in truth, because there is no truth in him" (John 8:44).

c. **2:10 "ten days":** This is an expression for a short period of time; we would say "a week and a half." Their faithfulness will not only bring them suffering and jail, but also a crown of life. Compare this to the fact that athletes in those days won not a trophy or medal, but a crown of flowers. Also, the city of Smyrna was built on a hill with a street of gold around the top which separated the high rent district from the poor. This circular golden street, from a distance, looked like a crown on the hill.

d. **2:11** The faithful of Smyrna will not be hurt by the "second death," which the last chapters of Revelation tell us is the final judgement of the condemned.

THINKING ALOUD

The Church faced a dual challenge: they had to establish the unique identity of Christian messianic faith distinct from their mother faith of Judaism, and they had to deal with their rejection as Jews who believed that Jesus is Messiah by the Jews who did not. The result was these sharp, bitter words of John to Smyrna.

We no longer face these challenges. We have two thousand years of distinction and autonomy as a faith, and these verses should in no way be the model for the Church's relationship to Judaism today. Our challenge is rather to maintain the uniqueness of the Christian message in the midst of competing "-isms" and philosophies, preserving its power to bring redemption by preserving the purity of the message.

3. The Letter to Pergamum (2:12-17)

To Pergamum   ¹²"To the angel of the church in Pergamum, write this:

" 'The one with the sharp two-edged sword says this: ¹³"I know that you live where Satan's throne is, and yet you hold fast to my name and have not denied your faith in me, not even in the days of Antipas, my faithful witness, who was martyred among you, where Satan lives. ¹⁴Yet I have a few things against you. You have some people there who hold to the teaching of Balaam, who instructed Balak to put a stumbling block before the Israelites: to eat food sacrificed to idols and to play the harlot. ¹⁵Likewise, you also have some people who hold to the teaching of [the] Nicolaitans. ¹⁶Therefore, repent. Otherwise, I will come to you quickly and wage war against them with the sword of my mouth.

¹⁷" ' "Whoever has ears ought to hear what the Spirit says to the churches. To the victor I shall give some of the hidden manna; I shall also give a white amulet upon which is inscribed a new name, which no one knows except the one who receives it." '

a.   **2:12**   Pergamum was the location of the regional court, signified by the presence of the *ius gladii* or "sword of justice." Therefore, Christ is described as the one who pronounces God's judgement, which is like a sword.

b.   **2:13**   Pergamum was the Roman provincial capital and the location of the first temple dedicated to worshipping the emperor as a god (during the time of Augustus). Because John sees Satan as the power behind the throne of Rome, and because that throne has its regional capital here, Pergamum is called the place "where Satan's throne is."

"**Antipas**," who was killed for his faith, is mentioned only here in the New Testament. Nothing else is known about him, except that he alone is called by the same words with which John describes Jesus, "faithful witness." What a high honor it was for Antipas to be described in the same way as our Lord! This suggests the existence of a whole other world of witnesses and saints in the early Church who are unknown to us, some of whom like Antipas may actually have been more significant in their own day than the ones who are canonized in Church history.

c. **2:14** In Numbers 22–24 the prophet Balaam disobeyed God by accepting King Balak's invitation to go curse Israel and its leader, Moses, who wished to cross Balak's land. Balaam is mentioned in several places in the Old Testament as a person who tried to bring harm to God's people. John says that the Christians in Pergamum are following Balaam in those who wanted to win their hearts by urging them to eat meat sacrificed to idols (false gods); to make matters worse, they are now following the Nicolaitans. Although this still does not tell us any more about who the Nicolaitans were, it does show us that it was not a strictly local group limited to Ephesus.

The question whether to eat this meat or not was a major controversy for St. Paul in Corinth (see 1 Cor 10). Paul knew that, because idols were false, there was nothing special about meat that had been offered to them and was later for sale at a discount in the market. However, he also knew the problems that would arise in people's minds if they saw Christians buying and eating this meat. Paul told the Corinthians to be their own judge whether to eat the meat or not, letting the conscience of others, whether they might be truly hurt by their eating or not eating, be their guide.

John favored a rigid separation between Christians and idol worshippers by strictly opposing eating the meat sacrificed to idols. He saw this as a sure path to worshipping the idols themselves.

d. **2:17** **"hidden manna"**: God fed the children of Israel in the desert with a bread-like substance which came to be called "manna." Jeremiah the prophet, according to Jewish legend, hid the ark of the covenant (which contained a jar of manna) in a cave until a time when Israel would be free again, a time of feasting at the banquet of God. Thus the banquet of God is contrasted with the banquet of those who eat the meat sacrificed to idols. The idea of a **"white amulet upon which is inscribed a new name"** comes out of ancient superstition. The ancients made amulets (charms) by taking a stone and inscribing on it the name of a god. The "white stone" represents an amulet with Christ's secret, new name written on it (see 19:16). The amulet may represent the Christians themselves, who, according to 14:1, will have the name of God and of Christ written on their foreheads. Only those who patiently obey Christ will know what it means to bear the name of Christ.

A note on the word "new." Revelation was originally written in Greek, as was the entire New Testament. In Greek there are two words for "new." One of them is *neos*, which means "brand new" or "fresh" as in "fresh dough," or "young" as in "young person." The other is *kainos*, which means "new and distinctive." Revelation uses this second word exclusively, referring to the believer's new name, Christ's new name, the new song, and the new Jerusalem. *Kainos* is used in the New Testament, including Revelation, to refer specifically to God's work of salvation, whereby a higher, more permanent order is reached. To make all things new is not to abolish all that was and put something entirely different and unheard of in its place. Rather, it is to make all things into something more, something not like they were, but still themselves. It represents a transformation which only God can accomplish. Thus, the "new name" represents one who is transformed by the power of God. To have Christ's new name written on one is to be transformed from the old, sinful self into his likeness.

THINKING ALOUD

John and Paul faced the challenge of guiding their non-Jewish followers into a faith and practice that was distinct from the religious culture around them. In a situation where a religion is firmly established, some degree of tolerance on the part of Christians may be acceptable, although this can easily lead to complacency. For the early Christians, any tolerance whatsoever blurred the lines of distinction between them and the surrounding culture, making faithfulness that much more difficult.

We might consider the attitudes of Paul and John, and consider how they address our spirit of tolerance or lack thereof for various practices of society in the Church today.

4. THE LETTER TO THYATIRA (2:18-29)

To Thyatira ¹⁸"To the angel of the church in Thyatira, write this:

" 'The Son of God, whose eyes are like a fiery flame and whose feet are like polished brass, says this: ¹⁹"I know your works, your love, faith, service, and endurance, and that your last works are greater than the first. ²⁰Yet I hold this against you, that you tolerate the woman Jezebel, who calls herself a prophetess, who teaches and misleads my servants to play the harlot and to eat food sacrificed to idols. ²¹I have given her time to repent, but she refuses to repent of her harlotry. ²²So I will cast her on a sickbed and plunge those who commit adultery with her into intense suffering unless they repent of her works. ²³I will also put her children to death. Thus shall all the churches come to know that I am the searcher of hearts and minds and that I will give each of you what your works deserve. ²⁴But I say to the rest of you in Thyatira, who do not uphold this teaching and know nothing of the so-called deep secrets of Satan: on you I will place no further burden, ²⁵except that you must hold fast to what you have until I come.

²⁶" ' "To the victor, who keeps to my ways until the end,
I will give authority over the nations.
²⁷ He will rule them with an iron rod.
Like clay vessels will they be smashed,

²⁸just as I received authority from my Father. And to him I will give the morning star.
²⁹" ' "Whoever has ears ought to hear what the Spirit says to the churches.' '

a. **2:18** Thyatira had a temple dedicated to Apollo, who was associated with the sun. Christ is the one whose eyes and feet blaze and shine like the sun.

b. **2:20 "the woman Jezebel":** John is using the name of the wife of King Ahab of Israel, who introduced the worship of false gods into Israel (1 Kgs 16:31-33), to describe those in Thyatira who believed that it was permissible to buy meat in the market which had been sacrificed to idols. John continues his very strict attitude towards this problem. This may lead us to think about how our actions appear to others.

c. **2:22-23** These verses contain a warning of strict punishment, including death, for those who continue to buy meat sacrificed to idols. For John this was an issue of spiritual life and death.

2:22 "those who commit adultery with her": John draws on the symbolism used in Hosea and elsewhere in the Old Testament, where Israel's unfaithfulness to God by worshipping false gods is called adultery or going to a prostitute.

2:23 "I am the searcher of hearts and minds": This phrase underscores the meaning of the eyes of flame.

2:24 "the so-called deep secrets of Satan": Either John is being sarcastic about those who claimed to know the deep secrets of God, or in the church of Thyatira there were members of a group (later called Gnostics) who claimed that spirituality consists of knowing the deep secrets of reality. The Church in all ages must remember that to be a faithful follower of Christ means living a life of simple obedience. It never merely means possessing deep intellectual knowledge of spiritual things, although individuals may be given this gift for the benefit of the Church.

d. Whereas Thyatira was perhaps the most unimportant town in the area, those who are victorious in Christ will be rulers of nations.

2:27 "He will rule them with an iron rod. Like clay vessels will they be smashed": These words refer to a prophecy about the Messiah in Psalm 2:8-9 in which he is promised authority over the nations.

2:28 "the morning star": This refers to Christ himself (see 22:16).

THINKING ALOUD

In every church at one time or another there arise strong and influential voices which call for compromise with culture and society. Their arguments usually include things such as, "We are too sophisticated for that to hurt us," "It will make us more attractive to more people," or "What will it hurt?"

These voices must be dealt with quickly and decisively, for they risk dragging the entire house down with them.

At the same time that we are dealing with these seditious voices, we must beware lest we discourage those who are seeking to do what is right and who don't have anything to do with the dissenters.

5. The Letter to Sardis (3:1-6)

3 To Sardis [1]"To the angel of the church in Sardis, write this:

" 'The one who has the seven spirits of God and the seven stars says this: "I know your works, that you have the reputation of being alive, but you are dead. [2]Be watchful and strengthen what is left, which is going to die, for I have not found your works complete in the sight of my God. [3]Remember then how you accepted and heard; keep it, and repent. If you are not watchful, I will come like a thief, and you will never know at what hour I will come upon you. [4]However, you have a few people in Sardis who have not soiled their garments; they will walk with me dressed in white, because they are worthy.

[5]" ' "The victor will thus be dressed in white, and I will never erase his name from the book of life but will acknowledge his name in the presence of my Father and of his angels.

[6]" ' "Whoever has ears ought to hear what the Spirit says to the churches." '

a. **3:1 "the seven spirits of God":** See comment on 1:4. This refers to God's sevenfold Holy Spirit.

"the seven stars": This relates specifically to Sardis because Sardis's acropolis (the highest, fortified part of a Greek city), a most impressive thing about the city, was located on a spur of a mountain. At night the vista of stars from that lofty place would have been impressive.

c. (Sections "b" and "c" are reversed in this letter.)

3:1 "you have the reputation of being alive, but you are dead": Another thing Sardis was known for was its necropolis, containing over a hundred burial mounds. The church there was as dead as the people buried in the city's cemetery.

3:2   "Be watchful": Both Cyrus the Great and Antiochus the Great were able to invade Sardis because it had failed to keep a sufficient guard on watch. Are the Christians of the city to repeat the folly of their ancestors, resting in blissful sleep as the Enemy approaches?

3:3   "like a thief": St. Paul had written forty years earlier in 1 Thessalonians 5:2, "For you yourselves know very well that the day of the Lord will come like a thief at night," and in 5:4, "But you, brothers, are not in darkness, for that day to overtake you like a thief." Ephesians 5:14 contains an ancient Christian hymnic version of Isaiah 60:1: "Awake, O sleeper, and arise from the dead, and Christ will give you light." The Christians at Sardis are urged to learn the lesson of history and of Scripture and maintain a perpetual vigil.

b.   **3:4   "a few . . . who have not soiled their garments; they will walk with me dressed in white"**: This refers to their baptismal garment, a white robe symbolizing purity, which was put on each person as they came up out of the baptismal waters. Those who kept themselves free of sin will inherit the eternal life symbolized by being "dressed in white."

d.   **3:5   "the book of life"**: Ancient Persian cities had tax rolls, and to be recorded therein meant citizenship in the city. The "book of life" is the citizenship roll book of the heavenly Jerusalem.

"I will . . . acknowledge his name in the presence of my Father and of his angels": Compare this with Luke 12:8, "I tell you, everyone who acknowledges me before others the Son of Man will acknowledge before the angels of God."

THINKING ALOUD

Sleepy self-satisfaction is one of the most dangerous enemies of the Church, for it does not announce itself loudly, nor does it have its vocal champions who campaign vigorously for it. When the Church has lived in a society such as the United States where over two hundred years of constitutional law have guaranteed its freedom, it is at high risk of contracting complacency. And, there are enough causes for the Church to champion without manufacturing them. In other words, the cure for complacency is not stirring up controversy where none is called for, but rather to be clear on our mission in the first place.

6. The Letter to Philadelphia (3:7-13)

To Philadelphia ⁷"To the angel of the church in Philadelphia, write this:

" 'The holy one, the true,
who holds the key of David,
who opens and no one shall close,
who closes and no one shall open,

says this:

⁸" ' "I know your works (behold, I have left an open door before you, which no one can close). You have limited strength, and yet you have kept my word and have not denied my name. ⁹Behold, I will make those of the assembly of Satan who claim to be Jews and are not, but are lying, behold I will make them come and fall prostrate at your feet, and they will realize that I love you. ¹⁰Because you have kept my message of endurance, I will keep you safe in the time of trial that is going to come to the whole world to test the inhabitants of the earth. ¹¹I am coming quickly. Hold fast to what you have, so that no one may take your crown.

¹²" ' "The victor I will make into a pillar in the temple of my God, and he will never leave it again. On him I will inscribe the name of my God and the name of the city of my God, the new Jerusalem, which comes down out of heaven from my God, as well as my new name.

¹³" ' "Whoever has ears ought to hear what the Spirit says to the churches." '

a. **3:7 "the holy one, the true"**: "Holy" is a Jewish title for God (Isa 6:3). "True" is used in other apocalyptic writings as well as here in Revelation not as the opposite of "false." Instead, it has the same meaning as in Psalm 146:6 where in the King James Version God is called the one "which keepeth true forever." In the NAB this is translated "Who keeps faith forever"; the same sense appears in English when we speak of someone being "true to his word." This is significant because it supports a key theme in Revelation. For John this revelation is not merely his meditations on the future of the Church in Asia Minor: it is a revelation given by God to Christ, which John is recording. Christ is the faithful witness, the one who keeps true, whose name is "Amen" (3:14), and whose word is totally reliable.

"who holds the key of David": Isaiah prophesied about Eliakim: "I will place the key of the house of David upon his shoulder; when he opens, no one shall shut, when he shuts, no one shall open" (Isa 22:22). This represents absolute authority either to admit or to bar people at the throne room of the king. Jesus has absolute authority to admit or refuse people before God's throne. Relate this to the fact that Philadelphia was the door, the gateway of communication and commerce from Sardis to the eastern part of Asia Minor.

b. **3:8 "I have left an open door before you"**: This refers to the Philadelphians' strategic location for going into the interior of Asia Minor and establishing new churches.

3:9 "the assembly of Satan who claim to be Jews but are not": See comment above on 2:9.

"I will make them come and fall prostrate at your feet": Compare this with Isaiah 60:14 in which the Lord's message is given to the Jews: "The children of your oppressors shall come, bowing low before you; All those who despised you [the Gentiles] shall fall prostrate at your feet." John reverses the message of Isaiah. Whereas the Jews expected that some day God would prove to the Gentiles that they, the Jews, are God's people, John says that instead God will prove to the Jews that the Christians are the true Israel.

We must keep in mind that both the Gospel of John and Revelation were written by a group of Christians who had suffered much from the Jews. While it is understandable that they would have a desire to see the tables turned, we must ask whether this should be *our* response to the Jews. Reading the Bible is like looking into a mirror. Sometimes we see Christ; we are seeing ourselves as we were meant to be, and we respond in thanksgiving and prayer. At other times we see ourselves as we truly are, and we respond with confession and repentance. Perhaps these verses about the Jews should be taken in this second way.

c. **3:10 "the time of trial that is going to come to the whole world to test the inhabitants of the earth":** Some refer to this as "the Great Tribulation," and include it in highly complex, carefully worked out schemes regarding the end of time. The word "trial" may also be translated "ordeal," and the "whole world" here means the whole non-Christian world. We know this because John uses the expression "the whole world" in 11:10, 12:9, and 16:14 of non-Christians, and nowhere does he use this expression to include Christians. The "time of trial" to which he is referring is the upcoming judgement which he believes the Roman Empire will very soon face. It will not be an ordeal for Christians, not because they will no longer be on the earth (as some interpreters say), but because they are not under God's judgement. The ordeal of non-Christians is the triumph of Christians in Revelation. The Christians' ordeal in John's time is the persecution they are suffering at the hands of the Jews and the Romans.

3:11 "crown": See comment above on 2:10.

d. **3:12 "a pillar in the temple of my God, and he will never leave it again":** This refers to the fact that ancient Philadelphia was so plagued with earthquakes that many residents preferred living in villages in the countryside. In God's temple Christians will stand solid as pillars, and will not have to run away because of danger.

"On him I will inscribe the name of my God and the name of the city of my God": In ancient times a person signed his name not with a pen, but with a signet in wax or soft clay. When the Roman soldiers sealed the tomb of Jesus, they did not place the stone door over the entrance; it was already there. Rather, they sealed it with a ribbon and the procurator's wax seal, which it was unlawful to break. Notice how "seal" is used in John's Gospel:

> **3:33** "Whoever does accept his testimony certifies that God is trustworthy" [a footnote in the NRSV says, for the word "certifies," "Greek: 'set a seal' "].

6:27 "For on him [the Son of Man] the Father, God, has set his seal."

We can see from this that in the writings named for John, "to seal" means "to certify or to grant rights and privileges to." Christ writes on them the names of God, the new Jerusalem, and his new name—the one only they who have been victorious can know. He does this to show that he who claims them for God marks them for citizenship in the kingdom of God as his own.

"the name of the city of my God, the new Jerusalem": In Revelation there is the *heavenly* Jerusalem, which comes down after the destruction of Rome and serves as the capital during the thousand-year reign of Christ, and the *new* Jerusalem, which is revealed after the old heaven and earth pass away and new ones take their place.

"my new name": Another significance of the idea of the new name is that Philadelphia's name had once been changed to "New Caesarea."

THINKING ALOUD

The Church must be constantly alert to the open doors Christ sets before it. Faced with hardships, we must remember that we have been claimed by God, who has signed us with his own name. This is reflected in the practice of marking a cross on a person's forehead at baptism. At this sealing in the baptismal service in the Episcopal Book of Common Prayer the priest says, "You are sealed by the Holy Spirit in baptism, and marked as Christ's own forever." With such a claim on our lives, how can we hesitate at the threshold of God's service?

7. The Letter to Laodicea (3:14-22)

To Laodicea 14"To the angel of the church in Laodicea, write this:

" 'The Amen, the faithful and true witness, the source of God's creation, says this: 15"I know your works; I know that you are neither cold nor hot. I wish you were either cold or hot. [16]So, because you are lukewarm, neither hot nor cold, I will spit you out of my mouth. [17]For you say, 'I am rich and affluent and have no need of anything,' and yet do not realize that you are wretched, pitiable, poor, blind, and naked. [18]I advise you to buy from me gold refined by fire so that you may be rich, and white garments to put on so that your shameful nakedness may not be exposed, and buy ointment to smear on your eyes so that you may see. [19]Those whom I love, I reprove and chastise. Be earnest, therefore, and repent.

[20]" ' "Behold, I stand at the door and knock. If anyone hears my voice and opens the door, [then] I will enter his house and dine with him, and he with me. [21]I will give the victor the right to sit with me on my throne, as I myself first won the victory and sit with my Father on his throne.

[22]" ' "Whoever has ears ought to hear what the Spirit says to the churches." ' "

a.   **3:14   "the Amen":** Here we have a Hebrew pun which draws from Isaiah 65:16, which in the Revised English Bible says, "God whose name is Amen," whereas the NRSV says, "the God of faithfulness." Which is it? As we have already seen, John almost always uses the full meaning of any Old Testament quote. So, when Jesus says that he is "the one called Amen," he is claiming to be God who is faithful, true to his word.

This ties in with the very next line, taken from 1:5, where Christ says that he is "the faithful and true witness." Christ is completely trustworthy, and all that he reports from the Father to his followers through John is reliable and true. (See comment about "true" above at 3:7.)

John adds: **"the source of God's creation."** The NRSV has "the origin [footnote: beginning] of God's creation." The key word is "beginning" and draws us back to the opening verse of the Gospel of John: "In the beginning was the Word." It was through Christ that God made the world, and it is in Jesus Christ that humanity discovers what it was to be all along and what it can yet become in him.

c.   (In the letter to the Laodiceans, there is no "b" section praising them for their good works.)

3:16 "you are lukewarm": Water flowed from the hot springs of Hieropolos to Laodicea, and by the time it got there it was only lukewarm. The tepid waters of that ancient stream provided a good jumping off place for jumping on the Laodiceans.

Unlike a church participating in or tolerating immoral activities, the Laodiceans were not doing anything, good or bad, which is a more dangerous condition than if they were openly immoral. The problem was that theirs was a rich city: a center of banking, textile industry, and learning. With all this economic and intellectual wealth, they were complacent and self-satisfied, having lost their original *enthusiasm* (meaning "to be filled with God"). Sound familiar? No wonder those who say that the seven letters to the churches represent the seven ages of the Church say that we are in the Laodicean age in the American church. The truth is that in all ages of the Church are found all seven kinds of churches here described.

3:17 "You say, 'I am rich and affluent and have no need of anything' ": This phrase is referring to Hosea 12:9 which says, "Though Ephraim [Israel = God's people] says, 'How rich I have become; I have made a fortune!' All his gain shall not suffice him for the guilt of his sin."

The Laodiceans make the same mistake as the ancient Israelites, which modern Americans also repeat: they think that their wealth is a sign of self-sufficiency and goodness, and the result is that it keeps them from seeing their spiritual poverty.

"poor, blind and naked": This is biblical sarcasm at its highest. These rich Laodiceans with their banks are really poor; these smart Laodiceans with their medical schools (which produced an eye salve renowned in the ancient world) are really blind; these industrious Laodiceans with their fine textile mills and clothing factories are really naked.

3:18 "I advise you to buy from me": This phrase recalls Isaiah 55:1b-2a: "Come, without paying and without cost, drink wine and milk! Why spend your money for what is not bread; your wages for what fails to satisfy?"

"buy from me gold refined by fire": The idea of being refined recalls Isaiah 48:10: "See, I have refined you like silver, tested you in the furnace of affliction." The Laodiceans are to seek a new spirit, tried in the crucible of hardship endured in the service of Christ and his people.

This new spirit will bear fruit and make them rich, enabling them to buy "white clothes." Laodicea was renowned for the glossy black fabric made there. In contrast the Laodiceans will live up to the meaning of their pure white baptismal robe and inherit the white robe of a spiritual body in heaven.

"nakedness": Beginning with the story of Adam and Eve in the garden (Genesis 3) nakedness has represented humanity's fallen, sinful condition.

"buy ointment to smear on your eyes": This refers to the powder which the Laodiceans produced as a major ingredient in Phrygian eye salve. Having true spiritual riches and being clothed with righteousness and eternal life opens one's spiritual eyes to see things as God would see them, putting everyone and everything in proper perspective. Note Paul's Letter to the Ephesians, which John would likely have known, 1:18: "May the eyes of [your] hearts be enlightened, that you may know what is the hope that belongs to his call, what are the riches of glory in his inheritance among the holy ones."

3:19 Christ indicates that his severe correction rises out of his love for them. See Proverbs 3:12: "For whom the LORD loves he reproves, and he chastises the son he favors." Love may be severe, but never cruel.

d. **3:20 "Behold, I stand at the door and knock":** The Greek wording here suggests that this is addressed not to the Laodicean church as a whole, but to its individual members. The love of Christ is both collective, for the Church, and individual, for each member of the Church.

"I will enter his house and dine with him": This is a sign of belonging to the same family, of fellowship. Eating together for people in the Middle East, both then and now, is a serious affair. An archaeologist and his son ate with a Jordanian sheik. They were there to ask him if they could dig near a burial site in his territory. After eating together the sheik pointed at the eight-year-old boy: "Now he is my son; and whenever he comes to Jordan he is to come to me and he will have a house and a woman and a horse." (The boy was excited about returning some day. Of course, being an eight-year-old he was excited about the horse.) If Christ comes in and eats with a person there is a familial bond which cannot be broken, and all he has is shared by the one with whom he eats. The church in Revelation receiving the most severe correction has received perhaps the most exalted promise of all, ''to sit with me on my throne'' (3:21).

THINKING ALOUD

It has been said, ''The church that takes a stand for nothing will fall for anything.'' The Laodiceans took self-satisfied complacency to a height never envisioned in Sardis. Their problem was that they thought they had it all, when all they had was second best.

How absurd is our storming of the gates of heaven with prayers and pleas for Christ when, if we would but remain still for a moment, we could hear his gentle knocking at our heart's door.

Section 2: The Seven Seals

Introduction (4:1–5:14)

III. God and The Lamb in Heaven

4　Vision of Heavenly Worship　[1]After this I had a vision of an open door to heaven, and I heard the trumpetlike voice that had spoken to me before, saying, ''Come up here and I will show you what must happen afterwards.'' [2]At once I was caught up in spirit. A throne was there in heaven, and on the throne sat [3]one whose appearance sparkled like jasper and carnelian. Around the throne was a halo as brilliant as an emerald. [4]Surrounding the throne I saw twenty-four other thrones on which twenty-four elders sat, dressed in white garments and with gold crowns on their heads. [5]From the throne came flashes of lightning, rumblings, and peals of thunder. Seven flaming torches burned in front of the throne, which are the seven spirits of God. [6]In front of the throne was something that resembled a sea of glass like crystal.

In the center and around the throne, there were four living creatures covered with eyes in front and in back. [7]The first creature resembled a lion, the second was like a calf, the third had a face like that of a human being, and the fourth looked like an eagle in flight. ⁸The four living creatures, each of them with six wings, were covered with eyes inside and out. Day and night they do not stop exclaiming:

"Holy, holy, holy is the Lord God almighty,
  who was, and who is, and who is to
    come."

⁹Whenever the living creatures give glory and honor and thanks to the one who sits on the throne, who lives forever and ever, ¹⁰the twenty-four elders fall down before the one who sits on the throne and worship him, who lives forever and ever. They throw down their crowns before the throne, exclaiming:

¹¹"Worthy are you, Lord our God,
  to receive glory and honor and power,
  for you created all things;
    because of your will they came to be and
      were created."

In chapters 4 and 5 John describes his vision of the heavenly court. There are many similarities between John's vision and that in Ezekiel chapter one. Our purpose here is to understand John's vision, not to do a detailed comparison with Ezekiel's, though you may wish to read the latter (see the comments above on 1:13-16).

Setting: In this section John is transported to heaven and reports what he sees.

4:1 "After this I had a vision": This expression, along with its shorter versions ("then I saw," etc.), occurs over and over in apocalyptic literature where the writers used it to describe the new conception of reality which they "saw" in their visions.

"an open door": This symbolizes the idea that heaven, normally closed to mortals, is being opened to admit John. In 19:11 all of heaven will be opened up.

"the trumpetlike voice that had spoken to me before": In 1:11ff. this was the voice of Christ. At times the voice is that of an unnamed angelic guide. Many of the elements of apocalyptic imagery are somewhat fluid, referring now to this, later to that. Keep in mind that what we have here is not a literal description, but a symbolic picture of spiritual realities.

"Come up here": John is invited to a loftier position to get a better view, to take, as it were, a heavenly journey. (This cannot in any way be construed as having anything whatsoever to do with the so-called rapture.)

4:2-3 "I was caught up in the spirit": John repeats the phrase he used in 1:10 in order to link that vision with this. The scene described here is in effect a continuation of that in chapter one.

"A throne was there in heaven, and on the throne sat one . . .": This is God, who is often described in the Bible like an ancient near-eastern king in his throne room surrounded by his courtiers. A contemporary American equivalent would be the President and his cabinet seated around the conference table as the President fields impromptu questions during a photo opportunity.

4:3 God's appearance is described impressionistically as resembling gleaming precious jewels. The **"halo as brilliant as an emerald"** is usually understood to symbolize eternal life (emerald green representing life, with the circular shape of the halo symbolizing eternity). It also recalls the rainbow God placed in the sky following the flood, sign of his covenant. There the symbolism derives from the ancient practice of a king hanging his bow on the wall of his throne room after winning a victory.

4:4 The **"twenty-four elders"** represent the twelve patriarchs (heads of the twelve tribes of Israel) and the twelve apostles. Their **"white garments"** indicate their status as holy ones of God having eternal life (recalling the white garment placed upon a person immediately after his or her baptism), and their **"gold crowns"** their positions of authority. All of God's people are continuously represented in the throne room of God, where they share in the government of God's kingdom with Christ, as he said they would.

4:5 "lightning . . . thunder": These have always been taken as witnesses to divine power. Job 36:32-33 states, "In his hands he holds the lightning, and he commands it to strike the mark. His thunder speaks for him and incites the fury of the storm.''

"seven torches . . . seven spirits": This is the same image used in chapter 1.

4:6 "a sea of glass like crystal": Exodus 24:9-11, when Moses takes Aaron and the elders of Israel atop Sinai to see and eat with God, says, ''Under his feet there appeared to be sapphire tilework, as clear as the sky itself'' (sapphire is a transparent, blue gemstone). Recall Genesis 1:6: ''Then God said, 'Let there be a dome in the middle of the waters, to separate one body of water from the other.' '' Ancient Hebrew cosmology (study of the structure and origin of the universe), limited as it was to observation with the naked eye, believed that the sky was blue because of the waters above the sky, which they understood to be a transparent dome. (The Hebrew word for ''dome'' used in Genesis 1:6 means ''something hammered as it were out of sheets of metal.'') Psalm 104:2b-3a says, ''You have spread out the heavens like a tent-cloth; you have constructed your palace upon the waters.''

What John is seeing (as he would expect to see up in heaven) are the waters above the sky, the sky itself a dome clear as crystal, and God's throne room built upon these waters. We face again the challenge of modern believers, to distinguish between the eternal truth of Scripture and the ancient understandings which sometimes form part of the vehicle which brings us that truth.

"four living creatures": This image comes directly from Ezekiel 1, although John modifies it somewhat. To understand the meaning of these four creatures we need to piece together the individual parts described by John and understand what they mean, and put them together as a whole (which is the way to understanding many of the visions in Revelation).

"covered with eyes": This image brings us back again to the vision of Zechariah involving the lampstand which was discussed in reference to chapter 1. Zechariah 4:10b says, ''These seven facets are the eyes of the LORD that range over the whole earth.'' The phrase ''covered with eyes'' indicates omniscience (the ability to see and know everything).

4:7 The four creatures may be said to represent:

> lion = wild animals
> bull = domesticated animals
> human = humans
> eagle = birds and fish

Therefore, the four creatures represent all living creatures, the four great classes of living things.

4:8 **"six wings"**: This recalls Isaiah's vision of heaven (Isa 6) and the six-winged creatures he saw around God's throne. Ezekiel called the four living creatures in his vision "cherubim" (this is the plural Hebrew form, the singular being "cherub"; as you can see, a cherub is nothing like the chubby little winged infants which decorate much of Renaissance art). These creatures do not merely symbolize the four classes of living creatures, but are also the all-seeing guardian protectors of all living creatures.

The four creatures also summarize the praises of all living things before God (Ps 150:6: "Let everything that has breath praise the LORD"). The first line of their song is that of the seraphim in Isaiah 6:3; the second line is drawn from the prologue to Revelation.

4:10 The four creatures are in an inner circle around the throne and represent all living creatures. The twenty-four elders are in an outer circle that specifically represents the people of God. The four seraphim lead the worship of God's people. In the preface to the Eucharistic Prayer for Epiphany are these words: "Now, with angels and archangels, and the whole company of heaven, we sing the unending hymn of your praise: Holy, holy, holy Lord, God of power and might . . ."

"they placed their crowns in front of the throne": This is a sign of their submission to God.

The Anglican hymnist Reginald Heber (1783–1826) incorporated many of these images in a hymn-poem which contains this verse:

> Holy, holy, holy! All the saints adore thee,
>   Casting down their golden crowns around the glassy sea;

Cherubim and seraphim falling down before thee
Which wert, and art, and evermore shalt be.

4:11 **"Lord and God"**: Domitian, the Roman emperor at
the time of John's writing, gave himself the title "Dominus
et Deus noster," which means "our Lord and God." John
takes the title and applies it where it truly belongs.

This is one of the many canticles (biblical songs not in the
psalms) which make Revelation such a musical book. God is
worthy of all the praise of all creation, because it was by his
free choice that he made all things.

THINKING ALOUD

While most of us have probably not witnessed a king holding court, we can find meaning in the idea that God is constantly mindful of all living things, and especially those whom
he has called to be his people. He created them, he has acted
to redeem them from humanity's sin, and he sustains them
with his Holy Spirit. God is aware of all that goes on in the
world, and "all your creatures praise you, and your faithful
servants bless you, confessing before the rulers of this world
the great Name of your only Son" (from the "Preface of A
Saint" in the Episcopal *Book of Common Prayer*).

> **5 The Scroll and the Lamb** ¹I saw a scroll in the right hand
> of the one who sat on the throne. It had writing on both sides
> and was sealed with seven seals. ²Then I saw a mighty angel
> who proclaimed in a loud voice, "Who is worthy to open
> the scroll and break its seals?" ³But no one in heaven or on
> earth or under the earth was able to open the scroll or to
> examine it. ⁴I shed many tears because no one was found
> worthy to open the scroll or to examine it. ⁵One of the elders
> said to me, "Do not weep. The lion of the tribe of Judah,
> the root of David, has triumphed, enabling him to open the
> scroll with its seven seals."
> ⁶Then I saw standing in the midst of the throne and the
> four living creatures and the elders a Lamb that seemed to
> have been slain. He had seven horns and seven eyes; these
> are the [seven] spirits of God sent out into the whole world.
> ⁷He came and received the scroll from the right hand of the
> one who sat on the throne. ⁸When he took it, the four living

creatures and the twenty-four elders fell down before the Lamb. Each of the elders held a harp and gold bowls filled with incense, which are the prayers of the holy ones. ⁹They sang a new hymn:

> "Worthy are you to receive the scroll
>   and to break open its seals,
>   for you were slain and with your blood
>   you purchased for God
>   those from every tribe and tongue, people
>   and nation.
> ¹⁰ You made them a kingdom and priests for our God,
>   and they will reign on earth."

¹¹I looked again and heard the voices of many angels who surrounded the throne and the living creatures and the elders. They were countless in number, ¹²and they cried out in a loud voice:

> "Worthy is the Lamb that was slain
>   to receive power and riches, wisdom and
>   strength,
>   honor and glory and blessing."

¹³Then I heard every creature in heaven and on earth and under the earth and in the sea, everything in the universe, cry out:

> "To the one who sits on the throne and to the
>   Lamb
>   be blessing and honor, glory and might,
>   forever and ever."

¹⁴The four living creatures answered, "Amen," and the elders fell down and worshiped.

5:1 "a scroll": Books in ancient times were most frequently long rolls of paper or parchment made from animal hide. Compare this passage with Jeremiah 36:2-3: "Take a scroll and write on it all the words that I have spoken to you against Israel, Judah, and all the nations, from the day I first spoke to you, in the days of Josiah, until today. Perhaps, when the house of Judah hears all the evil I have in mind to do to them, they will turn back each from his evil way, so that I may forgive their wickedness and their sin." Compare also with Ezekiel 2:9-10: "It was then I saw a hand stretched out to me, in which was a written scroll which he unrolled before me. It was covered with writing front and back, and written on it was: Lamentation and wailing and woe!''

The scroll John sees contains a description of human destiny, both regarding what humankind must endure in its history as a consequence of sin, and how God plans to redeem it.

"writing on both sides": The significance of its being written on both sides is simply that this scroll is thus linked with that in Ezekiel. (It was not unusual in ancient times for a scroll to be written on both sides to keep a lengthy message from requiring a long scroll, and to conserve paper.)

"sealed with seven seals": Such a roll was closed up by being tied with threads, each of which was sealed with wax. In Roman law a will was to be sealed with seven seals, each seal stamped with the signet of one of its seven witnesses. The will could not be put into effect until the seven seals were broken. Recalling that John is supposed to be in a trancelike state as he views all this, note Isaiah 29:11: ''For you the revelation of all this has become like the words of a sealed scroll. When it is handed to one who can read, with the request, 'Read this,' he replies, 'I cannot; it is sealed.' '' Also, in Daniel the prophet is told to seal up his vision, as it pertains to the future (8:26). Note especially Daniel 12:4: ''As for you, Daniel, keep secret the message and seal the book until the end time; many shall fall away and evil shall increase.''

Therefore, we have in this scroll in Revelation the declaration of the future of humankind, of the end of all things, sealed up until a time when evil will be growing in the world, a time such as that of John when the emperor is persecuting the people of God as they have never been persecuted before.

5:2 "Who is worthy?": To open the seals is not merely to reveal what is inside, it is to set in motion the events described. It is not for just anyone to do this.

5:4 "I shed many tears": John cries not because his curiosity goes unfulfilled regarding the contents of the scroll. To the contrary, he knows that the scroll contains God's plan for concluding and redeeming sinful human history, a history which for John has lost its meaning and can only be saved if it is brought to an end by a victorious Christ. He weeps because, until someone can be found who can open the seal, the process whereby God will bring final salvation is still on hold and John's community, God's people, go on suffering.

5:5 "the lion of the tribe of Judah": Jacob's last words in Genesis 49:9 call Judah a "lion's whelp" in a passage interpreted from before the time of Jesus as referring to the Messiah.

"the root of David": This phrase in the Greek actually says "the root of Jesse." It is from Isaiah 11:10 which also refers to the Messiah. Jesus, God's chosen Messiah, has won the victory through his death and resurrection, and so is worthy to initiate the sequence of events leading to the completion of human history and the final redemption of God's people.

5:6 "a Lamb": Here is a bit of irony. We are expecting to see the "lion of the tribe of Judah," and instead of a lion we see a lamb! Jesus won his victory not as a lion would, but as a sacrificial lamb.

He is "standing in the midst of the throne" because he is exalted at God's right hand (cf. Acts 2:33).

"seemed to have been slain": The risen Christ bears the marks of his crucifixion. The hymnist Charles Wesley wrote these lines:

> Those dear tokens of his passion still his dazzling body
>   bears,
> Cause of endless exultation to his ransomed worshippers;
> With what rapture gaze we on those glorious scars!

"seven horns": A ram's power is chiefly in his massive horns; "seven horns" represents complete divine power.

"seven eyes; these are the [seven] spirits of God sent out into the whole world": See the comment on 4:8.

5:8 "gold bowls filled with incense": The burning of incense has a double meaning. It represents purification, whereby something is signified as holy, and it symbolizes "the prayers of the holy ones." The Church throughout the centuries has envisioned the ministry of angels and of saints as offering to God the prayers of his people. Perhaps here we have a rudimentary reference to this. (Note that ''the holy ones'' may be translated ''the saints.'')

5:9 **''They sang a new hymn''**: Cf. Psalm 98, a psalm praising God who has won the victory and who comes to judge the earth.

''those from every tribe and tongue, people and nation'': This is from Daniel 7:14, where the Son of Man is commissioned by God to establish God's eternal kingdom on earth (see above at 1:13).

5:10 This verse refers back to 1:6, which in turn refers back to Exodus 19:6 which describes the destiny of God's people.

5:11-14 All the company and host of heaven continue their praises, drawn from Daniel 7:13-14. These verses are incorporated in the canticle *Dignus es* which is sung in the daily prayers of the Church. All of this worship in Revelation now leads to the opening of the seals, which initiates the final destiny of humankind.

THINKING ALOUD

There are many who would like both to know the future and to hold its reins. Yet such knowledge and power is not for everyone. Only the Lamb, whose obedient self-sacrifice on the cross won the victory over sin and death, has won that privilege.

Because of this all of God's people praise Christ the Lamb, and their prayers are presented before him day and night. If we want security about the future, we too must walk the way of the Lamb. Is that not what he meant when he said, ''Those who lose their life [and thereby sacrifice their future] for my sake will find it''?

The Opening of the Seven Seals

In this section the seven seals on the scroll of human destiny are opened. In a sense what we are receiving in this section is a preview of the remainder of the Book of Revelation: a description of the present state of human affairs, represented by what are called "The Four Horsemen of the Apocalypse"; the reassurance of the Church; and warnings and judgement against the wicked.

In this section we also see for the first time the use of an interlude between parts four and five of a section having seven parts. Also we see something that will occur again: the seventh part of the section introduces the next section.

IV. The Seven Seals, Trumpets, and Plagues, with Interludes

6 The First Six Seals ¹Then I watched while the Lamb broke open the first of the seven seals, and I heard one of the four living creatures cry out in a voice like thunder, "Come forward." ²I looked, and there was a white horse, and its rider had a bow. He was given a crown, and he rode forth victorious to further his victories.

³When he broke open the second seal, I heard the second living creature cry out, "Come forward." ⁴Another horse came out, a red one. Its rider was given power to take peace away from the earth, so that people would slaughter one another. And he was given a huge sword.

⁵When he broke open the third seal, I heard the third living creature cry out, "Come forward." I looked, and there was a black horse, and its rider held a scale in his hand. ⁶I heard what seemed to be a voice in the midst of the four living creatures. It said, "A ration of wheat costs a day's pay, and three rations of barley cost a day's pay. But do not damage the olive oil or the wine."

⁷When he broke open the fourth seal, I heard the voice of the fourth living creature cry out, "Come forward." ⁸I looked, and there was a pale green horse. Its rider was named Death, and Hades accompanied him. They were given authority over a quarter of the earth, to kill with sword, famine, and plague, and by means of the beasts of the earth.

The four horses and horsemen are adapted by John from Zechariah 6 where they represent patrols that God sends to the four corners of the earth. He also draws on Ezekiel 14:21 which refers to God's four deadly acts of judgement: sword, famine, wild animals, and pestilence. They also parallel what is called the "Little Apocalypse," a section in Mark, Matthew, and Luke in which Jesus tells his disciples about the end of history. Jesus tells them to expect wars between nations, famines, and death (Mark 13).

The four horsemen are also allusions to specific events in history. It is a characteristic of apocalyptic literature for the writer, who has taken the name of an ancient, credible author, to make a survey of history from the time of the author whose name he has appropriated to his own time so the reader can be placed within the context of history. He will also describe events in his own day as if they were prophecies (Daniel does this to such a degree that the writing of the second, apocalyptic part of Daniel may be dated as precisely as January or February, B.C. 164). He does all this not to deceive, but in order to lend credence to the prophecies he makes concerning events he foresees happening beyond his own day, and to help his readers see their place in these events.

We may view the four horsemen as representing the kinds of things that Christians must endure while awaiting final redemption and victory.

A. The White Horse (6:1-2)

6:2 "a white horse": A white horse is associated with a conquering general.

"its rider had a bow": The bow was the favorite weapon of the Parthian Empire, a nation to the east of the Roman Empire, located in what is now Iraq.

"given a crown": This is a reference to a legend alive at the time of John which said that the emperor Nero had not really committed suicide, but had fled east and would return at the head of a conquering Parthian army. (The victory of the eastern king Volagases over the Romans in 62 had already given the Romans the idea that an invasion from the east was possible.)

For John the premier antichrist is Domitian, the emperor who was persecuting the churches of Asia Minor at the time of the writing of Revelation. Because of the many similarities between Domitian and Nero, the first emperor to systematically persecute the Church, John uses Nero and things related to Nero to refer to Domitian.

Referring specifically in this verse to the old legend about Nero, John warns Christians that they will have to endure international strife.

B. The Red Horse (6:3-4)

6:4 **"Another horse came out, a red one"**: This represents the blood of warfare, which always follows the nationalistic sabre-rattling of the first horse. The "huge sword" symbolizes the rider's power to "take peace away" and bring war upon the earth.

C. The Black Horse (6:5-6)

6:5 **"a black horse"**: This horse represents famine, which is all too often a result of war.

"a scale": This is used to measure out the grain mentioned in the next verse.

6:6 There is a difference in price between "wheat" and "barley" because wheat is a finer, more expensive grain. Normally one could purchase anywhere from eight to sixteen times more grain with a day's wages, so this represents a time of scarcity, which is to be expected during and after war.

"But do not damage the olive oil or the wine": During the reign of Domitian there was a scarcity of grain, but there was more than enough wine. So, he issued an edict that no new vineyards be planted, and that some of the old vineyards be cut for land to farm grain. In Asia Minor there was such an uproar that the edict was not only cancelled but reversed: Domitian ordered punishment on anyone who destroyed their old vineyards.

John saw the irony of these political maneuverings, and it reminded him of old apocalyptic prophecies that, in the last days, there would be an abundance of grapes but a scarcity of grain because of political instability.

D. The Pale Green Horse (6:7-8)

6:8 "a pale green horse. Its rider was named Death":
It is indeed appropriate that the horse bearing Death should
be the color "chloros," the pale, sickly yellow-green that gave
its name to Chlorox. "Hades" was the mythical place where
departed spirits went.

"authority over a quarter of the earth": In general any fraction in apocalyptic literature indicates incompleteness. Thus,
this cycle of international unrest, war, famine, and death will
not result in the death of the entire human race.

E. The Fifth Seal (6:9-11)

[9]When he broke open the fifth seal, I saw underneath the
altar the souls of those who had been slaughtered because
of the witness they bore to the word of God. [10]They cried
out in a loud voice, "How long will it be, holy and true
master, before you sit in judgment and avenge our blood
on the inhabitants of the earth?" [11]Each of them was given
a white robe, and they were told to be patient a little while
longer until the number was filled of their fellow servants
and brothers who were going to be killed as they had been.
[12]Then I watched while he broke open the sixth seal, and
there was a great earthquake; the sun turned as black as dark
sackcloth and the whole moon became like blood. [13]The stars
in the sky fell to the earth like unripe figs shaken loose from
the tree in a strong wind. [14]Then the sky was divided like
a torn scroll curling up, and every mountain and island was
moved from its place. [15]The kings of the earth, the nobles,
the military officers, the rich, the powerful, and every slave
and free person hid themselves in caves and among mountain crags. [16]They cried out to the mountains and the rocks,
"Fall on us and hide us from the face of the one who sits
on the throne and from the wrath of the Lamb, [17]because
the great day of their wrath has come and who can with-
stand it?"

6:9 "underneath the altar": This is a place of refuge.
John's vision of heaven is modeled after the layout of the
Temple in Jerusalem, which harmonizes with the idea found

in Hebrews 8:5 that the earthly Temple is a copy and a shadow of the heavenly one where Christ entered. We also find in ancient Judaism a belief that the saints are under the altar in heaven.

This verse, added to the practice of ancient Christians who worshipped in the catacombs (Roman burial caves), influenced the practices of enclosing the relics of a saint in the altar in Roman Catholic churches, and of burying honored persons under the altar.

6:10 "How long . . . ?": In Zechariah's vision of the horsemen which John adapted, after seeing the horses the angel of the Lord says, " 'O Lord of hosts, how long will you be without mercy for Jerusalem . . . ?' . . . the Lord replied with comforting words" (Zech 1:12-13). Daniel asks an angel in 12:6, "How long shall it be to the end of these appalling things?" The answer to the question here in Revelation comes in 11:2.

Samuel John Stone incorporated these words from Revelation in his immortal hymn text, "The Church's One Foundation":

> Though with a scornful wonder men see her sore oppressed,
>   By schisms rent asunder, by heresies distressed;
> Yet saints their watch are keeping, their cry goes up,
>   "How long?"
> And soon the night of weeping shall be the morn of song.

6:11 "a white robe": This recalls the baptismal robe and symbolizes their immortal bodies.

"the number was filled of their fellow servants . . . who were going to be killed": This literally means, "When the roll of martyrs is complete." In Judaism, even before Christianity, it was believed that the end would come when the roll of the martyrs was completed. This does not necessarily mean that God is waiting for a magic number to be reached (although later Judaism interpreted it that way). Rather, the roll of martyrs is complete when, by their martyrdom, evil is overcome.

Thus John continues to preach the idea that the evil forces of this world are to be overcome not by taking up the sword, but by walking the path of martyrdom.

F. The Sixth Seal (6:12-17)

This seal is a preview of the end of history, taken from traditional descriptions such as those in the Gospels (see Matt 24:29).

6:12 "the whole moon became like blood": This happens in a total lunar eclipse, an event which is stirring and awe-inspiring today, and which must have been at times terrifying to the ancients.

6:14 "the sky was divided like a torn scroll curling up": This phrase occurs in Isaiah 34:4, where the prophet is describing God's judgement on the nations. John is portraying cosmic upheaval which he believes is directly caused by humanity's evil and God's judgement upon it.

6:15-17 The mighty of the earth, in the face of God's judgements, are reduced to snivelling heaps huddling in caves and wishing that the rocks would fall upon them. This description is from Hosea 10:8, where the prophet is describing God's judgement on Israel.

6:17 "the great day of their wrath": This verse, as well as 6:12, goes back to Joel 3:4: "The sun will be turned to darkness, and the moon to blood, at the coming of the day of the LORD, the great and terrible day." This "Day of the LORD" cannot be defined or described any better than it is in Isaiah 2:12: "For the LORD of hosts will have his day against all that is proud and arrogant, all that is high, and it will be brought low." He says that on that day people will "go into caverns in the rocks and into crevices in the cliffs, from the terror of the LORD" (2:21). Joel describes it as "a day of darkness and of gloom, a day of clouds and somberness!" (2:2). The ancient Latin hymn *Dies Irae* describes it this way:

> Day of wrath, O Day of mourning,
>   Day of prophets' bold forewarning,
> Heaven and earth in ashes burning.
>
> O what fear men's bosoms rendeth
>   When from heaven there descendeth
> The judge on whose sentence all dependeth.

This is the great and final day when God shall execute judgement, when no one shall be able to escape.

THINKING ALOUD

Christians then as now must live through a cycle of nationalistic strife, war, famine, and death. We often wonder how long God is going to delay setting right the injustices of the world. We have the same assurance the first readers of Revelation had: the assurance of eternal life given in our baptism. We know that by the willing self-sacrifice Christians everywhere make of their lives (their time, talents, and resources) we are bringing ourselves and our world ever closer to that day when all will be set right at last.

*Interlude: The Sealing of the 144,000 and
a Scene of Heavenly Worship (chapter 7)*

7 The 144,000 Sealed ¹After this I saw four angels standing at the four corners of the earth, holding back the four winds of the earth so that no wind could blow on land or sea or against any tree. ²Then I saw another angel come up from the East, holding the seal of the living God. He cried out in a loud voice to the four angels who were given power to damage the land and the sea, ³"Do not damage the land or the sea or the trees until we put the seal on the foreheads of the servants of our God." ⁴I heard the number of those who had been marked with the seal, one hundred and forty-four thousand marked from every tribe of the Israelites: ⁵twelve thousand were marked from the tribe of Judah, twelve thousand from the tribe of Reuben, twelve thousand from the tribe of Gad, ⁶twelve thousand from the tribe of Asher, twelve thousand from the tribe of Naphtali, twelve thousand from the tribe of Manasseh, ⁷twelve thousand from the tribe of Simeon, twelve thousand from the tribe of Levi, twelve thousand from the tribe of Issachar, ⁸twelve thousand from the tribe of Zebulun, twelve thousand from the tribe of Joseph, and twelve thousand were marked from the tribe of Benjamin.

Triumph of the Elect ⁹After this I had a vision of a great multitude, which no one could count, from every nation, race, people, and tongue. They stood before the throne and before the Lamb, wearing white robes and holding palm branches in their hands. [10]They cried out in a loud voice:

"Salvation comes from our God, who is
        seated on the throne,
    and from the Lamb."

[11]All the angels stood around the throne and around the elders and the four living creatures. They prostrated themselves before the throne, worshiped God, [12]and exclaimed:

"Amen. Blessing and glory, wisdom and
        thanksgiving,
    honor, power, and might
    be to our God forever and ever. Amen."

[13]Then one of the elders spoke up and said to me, "Who are these wearing white robes, and where did they come from?" [14]I said to him, "My lord, you are the one who knows." He said to me, "These are the ones who have survived the time of great distress; they have washed their robes and made them white in the blood of the Lamb.

[15]"For this reason they stand before God's throne
        and worship him day and night in his
            temple.
    The one who sits on the throne will shelter
        them.
[16] They will not hunger or thirst anymore,
        nor will the sun or any heat strike them.
[17] For the Lamb who is in the center of the throne will
        shepherd them
    and lead them to springs of life-giving
        water,
    and God will wipe away every tear from
        their eyes."

The theme of this section centers around the opening of the seals and the act of sealing, and it continues here. Remember that what we just saw in the first five seals was a preview of the remainder of the Book of Revelation.

7:1-3 The idea that angelic beings control various forces of nature is ancient. In these verses the angels that control the four winds are empowered to bring hurt upon land and sea as a warning of God's coming judgement. Before they do this they are told to wait by an angel from the east so that God's people can be sealed on the forehead.

7:3   "put the seal on the foreheads of the servants of our God": See the comment above on 3:12. John derives this idea from Ezekiel 9:4 where the Lord tells a cherub (an angelic creature) to "Pass through the city [Jerusalem] and mark an X on the foreheads of those who moan and groan over all the abominations that are practiced within it." Then in verse 5 the cherub is told to pass through the city and kill everyone who does not have the mark. Ezekiel seems to be drawing on Exodus, where the Hebrews marked lintels of their doorways with the blood of a lamb so the avenging angel of death would pass over them. Therefore we may interpret this marking in Revelation as a sign of God's claim on these people, showing that they are exempted from the judgement which God is about to bring upon the earth.

7:4   "one hundred and forty-four thousand marked from every tribe of the Israelites": Remember first that in Revelation "Israel" refers to spiritual Israel, the Church. This number, 144,000, is by no means a literal number, drawing 12,000 from each of the twelve tribes. This is a composite number made by combining other symbolic numbers. One thousand is one of the highest numbers in the Hebrew language, and is used to mean a very large number. There are twelve tribes, and twelve times 1,000 yields 12,000 in each tribe. Multiply this by twelve to get 144,000. Spiritual Israel (the Church) is built upon the foundation of the earthly Israel and its twelve tribes. John emphasizes this by listing the twelve tribes. The symbolism of the number 144,000 is that every single one of God's people who dies for his or her faith from every place on earth will be preserved and brought before God in heaven.

7:9   The **"great multitude, which no one could count"** are the 144,000, and since the crowd cannot be counted, this shows that 144,000 must be a symbolic number. Verse 14 will tell us that these are they who are coming through the great time of trouble, the great ordeal. This does not refer to the troubles which Christians in general must face, but to the ordeal which

John foresees occurring just before the end of history. In verses 1-8 the multitude was on earth, the Church Militant; here they are in heaven, the Church Triumphant.

John has now left his orderly progression in time to look ahead beyond the great time of ordeal to a vision of all the Church universal presented before God.

"from every race . . . and tongue": This goes back to Daniel 7 and Revelation 5 and illustrates the universality of God's people.

"white robes": These represent immortal, spiritual bodies, and recall the white robe given in baptism.

"palm branches": The palm branch was a symbol of independence and nationalistic victory from the time of the Maccabees, who won a relatively brief period of independence for the Jews before Rome invaded.

7:9-12 This great scene of heavenly worship reflects the joy of God's people as they anticipate the life of heaven.

7:14 **"These are the ones who have survived the time of great distress"**: The Greek text literally says, "These are the ones passing through the great ordeal," as if they are still arriving at the time of the vision. This identifies the 144,000, the great crowd, as the martyrs who have resisted compromise with evil and have paid for it with their lives.

"washed their robes and made them white in the blood of the Lamb": This refers to Isaiah 1:18, "Though your sins be like scarlet, they may become white as snow." It also refers to Zechariah 3:1-5 in which the priest Joshua has his filthy clothes changed to festal garments with the words, "See, I have taken away your guilt." Their clothes represent their immortal, spiritual bodies, therefore these are they who have received the gift of immortality because of their faith in the obedient, sacrificial death of Christ on their behalf.

7:15 **"will shelter them"**: The Greek text literally says that God will "spread his tent over them." This goes back to Exodus 40:19 and a time when the Israelites had just completed manufacturing the tent wherein they were to place the ark of the covenant: "He [Moses] spread the tent over the Dwelling . . ." This expression is seen only one other time in the Old

Testament. In Jeremiah 10:20 God describes the Exile of the
Jews and says that there will be "no one to pitch [spread] my
tent." Thus, when John says that God will spread his tent
over them, it does not merely mean that he will give them
shelter and protection; it means that his home, the tent of the
Old Testament, has become their home, in a symbolic but real
sense.

7:16-17   Notice how these verses are composed from various Old Testament sources:

7:16: "They will not hunger or thirst anymore, nor will the sun or any heat strike them.	Isaiah 49:10: "They shall not hunger or thirst, nor shall the scorching wind or the sun strike them."
7:17: "For the Lamb in the center of the throne will shepherd them and lead them to springs of life-giving water,	Psalm 23:1a, 2b: "The LORD is my shepherd . . ." "to safe waters you lead me."
"and God will wipe away every tear from their eyes."	Isaiah 25:8: "The Lord GOD will wipe away the tears from all faces."

This is a wonderful testimony of the comfort which awaits
God's people, and must surely have been an encouragement
to John's persecuted people, even as it is today in the face of
the death of a loved one.

THINKING ALOUD

   Our greatest fear today seems to be that of dying. We deny
death in every way we can, including our fascination with
youth and avoidance of the elderly. The interesting thing is
that in this section even the sealing of God did not protect these
martyrs from death. Jesus said, "And do not be afraid of those
who kill the body but cannot kill the soul; rather, be afraid of
the one who can destroy both soul and body in Gehenna"
(Matt 10:28). We do such things to avoid death that we miss
life. These martyrs in Revelation did not avoid physical death,
but having passed through it they discovered the joys of life
eternal.

G. *The Seventh Seal (8:1-5)*

8 The Seven Trumpets ¹When he broke open the seventh seal, there was silence in heaven for about half an hour. ²And I saw that the seven angels who stood before God were given seven trumpets.

The Gold Censer ³Another angel came and stood at the altar, holding a gold censer. He was given a great quantity of incense to offer, along with the prayers of all the holy ones, on the gold altar that was before the throne. ⁴The smoke of the incense along with the prayers of the holy ones went up before God from the hand of the angel. ⁵Then the angel took the censer, filled it with burning coals from the altar, and hurled it down to the earth. There were peals of thunder, rumblings, flashes of lightning, and an earthquake.

Here the opening of the last seal becomes the transition to the next section, the seven trumpets.

8:1 **"silence in heaven for about half an hour"**: While the worship of the saints and angels is wonderful and exalted, it falls silent so that the prayers of those yet suffering on earth (8:4) may be heard in heaven.

8:2 This verse sets the scene for the angels with the trumpets, but does so dramatically, interrupting the seventh seal for a moment to cue us as to what John sees happening during the silence.

8:3 **"another angel"**: This angel mediates the prayers of God's people; and since God's people the Church are known in Revelation as Israel, and Michael is said to be the guardian of Israel in the apocalyptic Book of Daniel and is identified as the mediator for God's people in other apocalyptic literature, this angel is generally agreed to be St. Michael the archangel.

"incense": In 5:8 we saw that incense represents the prayers of God's people. Therefore, for the angel to add incense, a sweet-smelling fragrance pleasing to God, to the prayers means that the prayers are pleasing to God.

8:5 This verse marks the beginning of the next set of actions, the blowing of the seven trumpets.

Section 3: The Seven Trumpets

Introduction

In the ancient world trumpets were used as a signal to alert the people to the coming of the king or of an enemy army, to summon them to hear a proclamation, or as a warning. They were also used in battle to signal troops and to terrorize the enemy.

Here John is using them to herald the warnings of God's coming judgement on the wicked Roman Empire. The incomplete nature of the destruction which accompanies the sounding of the trumpets indicates that they are warnings of judgement and not the judgements themselves. They are highly reminiscent of the plagues of Egypt, which were also warnings from God for Pharaoh to repent. The symbolism of Israel captive in Egypt is paralleled in Revelation with the Church held captive by the Roman pharaoh Domitian.

A. The First Trumpet: A Plague against the Land (8:7)

The First Four Trumpets ⁶The seven angels who were holding the seven trumpets prepared to blow them.

⁷When the first one blew his trumpet, there came hail and fire mixed with blood, which was hurled down to the earth. A third of the land was burned up, along with a third of the trees and all green grass.

⁸When the second angel blew his trumpet, something like a large burning mountain was hurled into the sea. A third of the sea turned to blood, ⁹a third of the creatures living in the sea died, and a third of the ships were wrecked.

¹⁰When the third angel blew his trumpet, a large star burning like a torch fell from the sky. It fell on a third of the rivers and on the springs of water. ¹¹The star was called "Wormwood," and a third of all the water turned to wormwood. Many people died from this water, because it was made bitter.

¹²When the fourth angel blew his trumpet, a third of the sun, a third of the moon, and a third of the stars were struck, so that a third of them became dark. The day lost its light for a third of the time, as did the night.

¹³Then I looked again and heard an eagle flying high overhead cry out in a loud voice, "Woe! Woe! Woe to the inhabitants of the earth from the rest of the trumpet blasts that the three angels are about to blow!"

"hail and fire mixed with blood": This suggests a severe, killer thunderstorm with very large hail and dangerous lightning. It recalls the seventh plague against Egypt, that of thunder and hail which burned with fire.

"a third": Fractions in apocalyptic literature denote incompleteness; these are warnings, not judgements. This fraction, one-third of humans killed, represents an escalation from the fourth seal, where it was only one-fourth.

B. The Second Trumpet:
A Plague against the Sea (8:8-9)

8:8 "something like a large burning mountain": This suggests a great volcano such as Etna or Vesuvius. Note Jeremiah 51:25, part of a prophecy against Babylon (a city that enslaved the Jewish nation in B.C. 587 and will be used by John as a symbol for Rome): "Beware! I am against you, destroying mountain, destroyer of the entire earth, says the LORD; I will stretch forth my hand against you, roll you down over the cliffs, and make you a burnt mountain.

"the sea": As the Nile was to Egypt for transportation and commerce, so the Mediterranean Sea was to the Roman Empire.

"turned to blood": This calls to mind the first plague against Egypt.

8:9 In Egypt the fish in the river died; so here "a third of the creatures living in the sea died."

C. The Third Trumpet:
A Plague against the Fresh Waters (8:10-11)

8:10 "a large star": This is an image borrowed by John from Isaiah (14:12-20), who in turn borrowed it from an ancient Canaanite myth. In the myth the morning star Helal seeks to storm the heights of heaven and is thrown down. In Isaiah this is applied to the king of Babylon. For a second time John has applied a prophecy concerning the downfall of Babylon to Rome. The fall of Rome's star signals its impending doom.

8:11 **"wormwood"**: This goes back to Jeremiah 9:14, "See now, I will give them wormwood to eat and poison to drink." This trumpet involves the fresh waters as the second trumpet affected the seas.

D. The Fourth Trumpet:
A Plague against the Heavens (8:12)

This plague recalls the darkness which covered Egypt, as well as the statement of Jesus in Mark 13:24, "But in those days after that tribulation the sun will be darkened and the moon will not give its light."

It misses the point to debate whether **"They each lost a third of their light"** means that they shone one third less time each day or with one third less intensity. The point is that God is warning Rome to repent by means of a noticeable dimming of the heavenly sources of light upon which the ancients depended so heavily.

THINKING ALOUD

John, like Moses, interpreted various natural disasters as warnings from God. This idea can cause us problems today. Natural disasters have a terrible habit of being rather unselective when it comes to afflicting both the guilty, such as pharaohs and emperors, and the innocent, such as babies and young children.

The artist is in the art displayed; God is seen in his creation. If what we see in creation is warning against judgement, perhaps that is the side of God our guilty minds lead us to see and, indeed, need to see. A person within the will of God would see in the same activity of creation the might, the power, and the grace of God. The objective reality is perceived subjectively. This is a great mystery, and bespeaks our need of the prophets, who make clear the mind of God to us.

Interlude 1:
Announcement of the Three Woes (8:13)

In the last section we had the four horsemen as a group, then the other three seals. Here the first four trumpets are grouped as natural disasters and separated from the last three which are about warfare between the nations.

John in this section describes natural calamities, inner decay, and invasion as bringing down the Roman Empire. Edward Gibbon in *The Decline and Fall of the Roman Empire* lists the very same things.

8:13 "eagle": The eagle's announcement indicates that the next three trumpet blasts will each bring a woe upon the people. An alternative translation for "eagle" is vulture, which would lend some interesting connotations here.

E. The Fifth Trumpet: The First Woe (9:1-12)

9 The Fifth Trumpet ¹Then the fifth angel blew his trumpet, and I saw a star that had fallen from the sky to the earth. It was given the key for the passage to the abyss. ²It opened the passage to the abyss, and smoke came up out of the passage like smoke from a huge furnace. The sun and the air were darkened by the smoke from the passage. ³Locusts came out of the smoke onto the land, and they were given the same power as scorpions of the earth. ⁴They were told not to harm the grass of the earth or any plant or any tree, but only those people who did not have the seal of God on their foreheads. ⁵They were not allowed to kill them but only to torment them for five months; the torment they inflicted was like that of a scorpion when it stings a person. ⁶During that time these people will seek death but will not find it, and they will long to die but death will escape them.

⁷The appearance of the locusts was like that of horses ready for battle. On their heads they wore what looked like crowns of gold; their faces were like human faces, ⁸and they had hair like women's hair. Their teeth were like lions' teeth, ⁹and they had chests like iron breastplates. The sound of their wings was like the sound of many horse-drawn chariots racing into battle. ¹⁰They had tails like scorpions, with stingers; with their tails they had power to harm people for five

months. ¹¹They had as their king the angel of the abyss, whose name in Hebrew is Abaddon and in Greek Apollyon.

¹²The first woe has passed, but there are two more to come.

9:1 "star": This must be an angelic being, especially considering that the term *fall* is usually used in apocalyptic literature when a star is representing an angel. Such representation goes back to the ancient idea (which we saw before and will see again in Revelation) that angelic powers controlled the various forces and heavenly bodies in nature.

"the abyss": This is the pit, called "Sheol" by the Hebrews and "Tartarus" in Greek mythology (2 Pet 2:4 uses the actual word "Tartarus" in the Greek text). It is the place below the world of the dead (the world of the dead was called "Hades") where the wicked are punished—hell's basement, so to speak. The apocryphal book 1 Enoch identifies the angel having the key to Tartarus as Uriel. The New Testament has borrowed this concept to describe the place where the fallen angels are imprisoned (see 1 Pet 3:19 and Jude 6).

9:2 This "smoke" is consistent with ancient conceptions of the abyss. The woe John is about to describe reminds us of the plague of locusts in Egypt. John also draws from the apocalyptic Old Testament writer Joel, who described a swarm of destructive locusts as a day of clouds and thick darkness.

9:3-6 These are unnatural "locusts" because they are not to "harm the grass of the earth or any plant or tree" which, of course, is the natural diet of locusts. Rather, they are to torment those not previously marked on the foreheads with "the seal of God." They make them suffer "five months" because this was the natural life span of a locust. The locusts' wounds were "like that of a scorpion," whose sting is painful but rarely fatal. These locusts make the people suffer but will not kill them. The suffering they cause will be so bad that "these people will seek death but will not find it."

9:7 "The appearance of the locusts was like that of horses ready for battle": Joel describes locusts by saying that "Their appearance is that of horses; like steeds they run" (Joel 2:4).

"They wore what looked like crowns of gold": This locust swarm represents something connected with royalty. It is not royalty itself, for these were only *like* gold crowns. This signifies that these locusts attack with imperial authority.

"human faces": John is not representing here some impersonal force: evil has a human face, and these locusts represent an evil of human doing. As we accumulate clues we will draw closer to naming this evil.

9:8 The first part of this verse is reminiscent of an Arabic proverb that says that the antennae of locusts look like a maiden's hair. The second part comes directly from Joel 1:6. These are further descriptions of this monstrous evil which afflicts humankind.

9:9 Additional descriptions of the locusts drawn from Joel.

9:10 This is but a reiteration of what was said in 9:3 and 5.

9:11 **"They had as their king the angel of the abyss, whose name in Hebrew is Abaddon and in Greek Apollyon":** Now we come to the key to identify this horrible evil. The Hebrew word *Abaddon* means "destruction," etymologically, and was used as another word for death or the place of the dead (Sheol, Hades). It is true that the Greek Old Testament translated *abaddon* as *apoleia*, but John says that the angel's Greek name is not *apoleia* (the usual Greek word for "destroyer") but *Apollyon*. *Apollyon*, spelled this way, occurs only here in ancient Greek literature, meaning that this is a form of the word which John has constructed for use in this verse. Here is the key to the identity of these locusts. *Apollyon* is a deliberate pun on the name of the god Apollo, who was symbolized by (among other pests) the locust!

Thus, John has been describing the suffering and inner decay of the Roman Empire caused by the selfishness and debauchery brought on by its idolatry. Like locusts that eat crops and bring destruction upon an agrarian society, these "locusts from Hell" representing Roman idolatry have eaten away at the heart of Roman society until it is near collapse. Under imperial protection and endorsement the religion of Rome and its emperor also brought suffering to Christians and to many others in the eastern provinces of the Empire.

9:12 John is saying, "If you think that was bad, just wait—there's more!"

THINKING ALOUD

When the average American thinks of idolatry, a village ritual in India probably comes to mind. If, on the other hand, we use Paul Tillich's definition of God as "Ultimate Concern," we realize that Wall Street (just to take one example) is full of idolaters who sacrifice even their own marriages in the name of making money. We may be sophisticated, but idolatry can match our sophistication.

F. The Sixth Trumpet: The Second Woe (9:13-21)

The Sixth Trumpet [13]Then the sixth angel blew his trumpet, and I heard a voice coming from the [four] horns of the gold altar before God, [14]telling the sixth angel who held the trumpet, "Release the four angels who are bound at the banks of the great river Euphrates." [15]So the four angels were released, who were prepared for this hour, day, month, and year to kill a third of the human race. [16]The number of cavalry troops was two hundred million; I heard their number. [17]Now in my vision this is how I saw the horses and their riders. They wore red, blue, and yellow breastplates, and the horses' heads were like heads of lions, and out of their mouths came fire, smoke, and sulfur. [18]By these three plagues of fire, smoke, and sulfur that came out of their mouths a third of the human race was killed. [19]For the power of the horses is in their mouths and in their tails; for their tails are like snakes, with heads that inflict harm.

[20]The rest of the human race, who were not killed by these plagues, did not repent of the works of their hands, to give up the worship of demons and idols made from gold, silver, bronze, stone, and wood, which cannot see or hear or walk. [21]Nor did they repent of their murders, their magic potions, their unchastity, or their robberies.

9:13 Remember that John pictures heaven as the real temple, of which the earthly Temple was a copy. This is presumably the same altar under which the saints were seen in an earlier chapter. The voice from the altar represents divine command.

9:14 The Euphrates was the border between the Roman and the Parthian Empires. On the Parthians, see the comment above on 6:1-2. This was a site of constant border skirmishes and raids.

"four angels": The number four may derive from the four angels who held back the wind, which draws on the idea of angels controlling the forces of nature. Otherwise, the source of this specific idea of the "four angels who are bound at the banks of the great river Euphrates" is unknown. However, in general John is probably drawing on the apocalyptic book 1 Enoch which contains this verse: "And in those days the angels shall return and hurl themselves to the East upon the Parthians and Medes. They shall stir up the kings so that a spirit of unrest shall come upon them." John envisions the divine command being given for this to take place.

9:15 This verse suggests that God is following a plan carefully worked out for this very time. The fraction "a third" is partial destruction, representing a warning, not a judgement.

9:16 **"two hundred million"**: The Greek here literally says "two myriads of myriads." This means in effect "more than can be numbered."

9:17 The colors of the cavalry troops' uniforms reflect the colors of fire, smoke, and sulphur. Fire and sulphur (known from the King James Version as "fire and brimstone") were ancient means of divine purification, as when fire and sulphur rained down upon the sinful cities of Sodom and Gomorrah. This army is modeled after the Parthian armies, but the fire-breathing horses and the angels that released them denote that, as in the previous trumpet we had the "locusts from hell," here we have the "horses from hell," that is, evil forces at work in the world.

9:19 "Mouths" and "tails" refer to the Parthian tactic of using their excellent mounted archers to fire at the enemy both as they rode toward them and also after they had passed, all while at full gallop, turning in the saddle and shooting backwards.

9:20-21 These verses provide confirmation that the trumpets are warnings for the wicked to turn away from their evildoing. The problem is that the wicked are not heeding the warning.

THINKING ALOUD

Throughout the Old Testament the prophets viewed the nations as God's instruments in bringing blessing and punishment upon his people. While moderns might have a difficult time with the kind of determinism that sees entire countries acting as if they were God's puppets, the principle is the same as with the natural disasters above. People are God's creatures, too; and what does the doctrine of the Holy Trinity teach us but that God is in some sense a social being? Therefore, if we are watching and listening, we may see in the actions of other nations what God wants us to see for our own salvation.

Interlude 2a: The Little Scroll (ch. 10)

10 The Angel with the Small Scroll ¹Then I saw another mighty angel come down from heaven wrapped in a cloud, with a halo around his head; his face was like the sun and his feet were like pillars of fire. ²In his hand he held a small scroll that had been opened. He placed his right foot on the sea and his left foot on the land, ³and then he cried out in a loud voice as a lion roars. When he cried out, the seven thunders raised their voices, too. ⁴When the seven thunders had spoken, I was about to write it down; but I heard a voice from heaven say, "Seal up what the seven thunders have spoken, but do not write it down." ⁵Then the angel I saw standing on the sea and on the land raised his right hand to heaven ⁶and swore by the one who lives forever and ever, who created heaven and earth and sea and all that is in them, "There shall be no more delay. ⁷At the time when you hear the seventh angel blow his trumpet, the mysterious plan of God shall be fulfilled, as he promised to his servants the prophets."

⁸Then the voice that I had heard from heaven spoke to me again and said, "Go, take the scroll that lies open in the hand of the angel who is standing on the sea and on the land." ⁹So I went up to the angel and told him to give me the small scroll. He said to me, "Take and swallow it. It will turn your stomach sour, but in your mouth it will taste as sweet as honey." ¹⁰I took the small scroll from the angel's hand and swallowed it. In my mouth it was like sweet honey, but when I had eaten it, my stomach turned sour. ¹¹Then someone said to me, "You must prophesy again about many peoples, nations, tongues, and kings."

10:1 "mighty angel": This angel may be St. Gabriel the archangel, whose name means "Mighty One of God." The "halo" recalls the rainbow surrounding God's throne. It is caused by the light of the angel's face shining on the "cloud" with which he was covered. His "face like the sun" recalls the description of Christ in chapter 1. His "feet [legs] like columns of fire" calls to mind the angel that stood in and rose from the flames of the sacrificial offering made by Samson's father Manoah. That angel brought the annunciation of the birth of Samson, even as Gabriel brought the annunciation of the birth of our Lord to the Blessed Virgin Mary.

10:2 "a small scroll": This scroll is described in much the same way as the one in chapter 5; both descriptions are taken from Ezekiel 2:9-10. John is told to eat it as Ezekiel was. The two scrolls are definitely different here in Revelation. The scroll with the seven seals was the scroll of human destiny in a general sense. The small scroll describes specifically what will happen soon, from John's standpoint. Its contents are revealed in 11:1-13: the preservation of God's people from spiritual harm, the emergence of the beast who murders the people of God, the resurrection of the dead, and the destruction of Rome. This will then be expanded and described in detail in the remainder of Revelation.

"his right foot on the sea and his left foot on the land": This represents the global import of the message in the scroll. This phrase, as well as the phrase in 10:5, in which he "raised his right hand to heaven," recalls a vision in Daniel 12:5-7 in which two angels appear, one on either bank of a stream. The one upstream "raised his right hand and his left hand toward heaven."

10:3 The description of Gabriel's voice suggests that he speaks with the voice of God, as a true mediator/messenger would speak ("angel" means "messenger").

"as a lion roars": Amos 3:8 compares God speaking to his prophet with a lion roaring.

"the seven thunders raised their voices, too": In Psalm 29:3-9 the expression "the voice of the Lord" is repeated seven times, followed each time by a description of the power of his voice.

10:4 "do not write it down": The same voice which earlier told John to write down what he saw now tells him not to write. Apocalyptic books typically contain visions that are sealed or which are known only to the seer. It is not known what the seven thunders might be; perhaps John's readers already knew what they were and he only needed to refer to them by title; or, as the text says, they are simply prophetic visions which John saw but was restrained from writing. (Besides, including these visions would have spoiled the design of the book, which, as it stands, has seven sections. Perhaps it was really the voice of his editor!)

10:7 "the mysterious plan of God": This phrase in Greek says literally "the mystery of God." The ways of God are mysterious even to God's most devoted followers. Isaiah 55:9 says, "As high as the heavens are above the earth, so high are my ways above your ways and my thoughts above your thoughts." Yet, mysterious as are the ways of God, they are not random or purposeless: God has a plan. John and his followers will not need to wait much longer for this plan, activated by the opening of the seven seals, to be brought to pass.

10:9 "It will turn your stomach sour, but in your mouth it will taste as sweet as honey": The order here would seem to be reversed. Ordinarily one would first taste something, then become sick. The scroll contains primarily a description of the suffering of God's people, which will make John sick to his stomach, and secondarily a description of the destruction of Rome, which will be sweet to his lips.

10:11 John is about to tell us what the little scroll contains.

THINKING ALOUD

Knowledge of God's intentions regarding nations and peoples is a heavy burden indeed. Accepting the responsibility of being a prophet can give one a stomach ache, but the word of God is sweet as honey as well. The good news has its dark side, the news about the consequences of continuing in sinful behavior, which is ultimately self-destructive. But to be faithful to God, the good news must be proclaimed in its entirety.

Interlude 2b:
The Contents of the Little Scroll (11:1-14)

11 The Two Witnesses ¹Then I was given a measuring rod like a staff and I was told, "Come and measure the temple of God and the altar, and count those who are worshiping in it. ²But exclude the outer court of the temple; do not measure it, for it has been handed over to the Gentiles, who will trample the holy city for forty-two months. ³I will commission my two witnesses to prophesy for those twelve hundred and sixty days, wearing sackcloth." ⁴These are the two olive trees and the two lampstands that stand before the Lord of the earth. ⁵If anyone wants to harm them, fire comes out of their mouths and devours their enemies. In this way, anyone wanting to harm them is sure to be slain. ⁶They have the power to close up the sky so that no rain can fall during the time of their prophesying. They also have power to turn water into blood and to afflict the earth with any plague as often as they wish.

⁷When they have finished their testimony, the beast that comes up from the abyss will wage war against them and conquer them and kill them. ⁸Their corpses will lie in the main street of the great city, which has the symbolic names "Sodom" and "Egypt," where indeed their Lord was crucified. ⁹Those from every people, tribe, tongue, and nation will gaze on their corpses for three and a half days, and they will not allow their corpses to be buried. ¹⁰The inhabitants of the earth will gloat over them and be glad and exchange gifts because these two prophets tormented the inhabitants of the earth. ¹¹But after the three and a half days, a breath

of life from God entered them. When they stood on their feet, great fear fell on those who saw them. [12]Then they heard a loud voice from heaven say to them, "Come up here." So they went up to heaven in a cloud as their enemies looked on. [13]At that moment there was a great earthquake, and a tenth of the city fell in ruins. Seven thousand people were killed during the earthquake; the rest were terrified and gave glory to the God of heaven.

[14]The second woe has passed, but the third is coming soon.

11:1 "a measuring rod": A reed cut to a specific length was used in those days in much the same way we would use a yardstick or a tape measure.

"measure the temple of God and the altar": Measuring is a form of assessing and claiming. This temple is neither the one in heaven, nor the one in Jerusalem (it was destroyed a quarter century before Revelation was written). The temple and **"those who are worshiping in it"** symbolize the Church, God's people present in the world.

11:2 "exclude the outer court of the temple . . . it has been handed over to the Gentiles": The model for this image is the Jerusalem Temple. It had an inner courtyard, the Court of Israel, where the people of God worshipped, and an outer courtyard, the Court of the Nations (or, literally, Gentiles) where non-Jews could worship. It is the inner courtyard of God's people that is being claimed by God and placed under his protection as symbolized by the measuring.

"forty-two months": The apocalyptic second half of Daniel symbolically describes the terrible rule of Antiochus IV Epiphanes over the Jewish people in the B.C. 160s. In the power vacuum left by the death of Alexander the Great, the Syrian general Antiochus tried to invade Egypt. Failing, he took his anger out on Israel, forcing them at the point of the sword to abandon the practice of the Jewish faith and to adopt Greek practices instead. As an example of the cruelty and horror he imposed, Antiochus once arrested seven sons and their mother and ordered each son, one by one, to eat pork. One by one the sons refused, and one by one he had them put to death by the sword in front of their mother. Finally, he killed her as well. He set up an altar to Zeus on the altar of burnt offering in the Temple, an act called in the Bible ''the abomination of desolation.''

Antiochus's reign of terror lasted roughly three and a half years, from B.C. 167 to 164, the year he died. It came to represent a time of the most horrible persecutions and suffering, with the number three and a half serving as a shorthand reference to it. The angel in Daniel 12, who parallels Gabriel in Revelation 10:5, told Daniel that the troubles besetting God's people would last ''a time, two times, and half a time'' (literally, ''a time, times and a half''). This is taken to mean three and a half years, or ''forty-two months.''

Thus in Revelation three and a half years (and any numerical equivalent thereof in days or in months) represents a time of great ordeal.

11:3 ''**my two witnesses**'': These will be described beginning in the next verse. They wear **''sackcloth,''** which is a fabric much like burlap, used to make grain bags and worn to demonstrate repentance or mourning. They wear it because of the seriousness of their message and because they are mourning the sinful state of humankind. There are ''two'' of them because the Law of Moses required a minimum of two witnesses to prove a person's guilt in capital cases.

''twelve hundred and sixty days'': This is equivalent to the forty-two months (three and a half years) in 11:2.

11:4 ''**two olive trees**'': In the vision in Zechariah 4, which is the background for the vision of the seven candlesticks at the beginning of Revelation, the two olive trees are described by the angel as ''the two anointed ones who stand by the Lord of the whole earth'' (4:13), that is, Zerubbabel the governor and Joshua the high priest. Here in Revelation they symbolize Moses and Elijah, as seen in verse 6 below, and they are ''two lampstands'' because they are Israelite bearers of the divine light to God's people directly from God himself.

11:5 ''**the fire which comes out of their mouths**'': This represents the words of judgement they shall speak which, like the fire out of heaven raining down on wicked Sodom and Gomorrah, will destroy the enemy.

11:6 **"The power to close up the sky and to keep rain from falling"** refers to 1 Kings 17:1ff., in which Elijah withholds rain from Israel as a warning of God for them to repent. The **"water to blood"** and **"all kinds of terrible troubles"** represent Moses bringing the plagues on Egypt. Moses and Elijah were the first and last of the prophets. Elijah was the last because, according to Malachi 3:23 (4:5 in Protestant Bibles), the Lord will "send you the prophet Elijah before the great and terrible day of the LORD comes."

11:7 **"The beast"** has yet to be described. He represents political power that opposes and seeks to silence "God's message" and temporarily at least seems to succeed.

11:8 **"Their corpses will be left lying in the streets"**: Displaying the bodies of the defeated in a shameful way was an ancient custom.

"the . . . great city": Nineveh, wicked capital of Assyria which invaded and deported the people of Israel, is called "that great city" four times in the Book of Jonah. In Revelation this expression means Rome, a great city which, like Nineveh, was wicked and which invaded and (in the Diaspora) deported God's people.

"where their Lord was nailed to the cross": In what sense was Christ nailed to the cross in Rome? It was under the authority of a Roman procurator that Jesus was executed in a Roman provincial capital city.

"spiritually": This word is sometimes also translated "allegorically" (RSV) and "prophetically" (NRSV), meaning that the city in a religious, not literal, sense is "like the city of Sodom or the country of Egypt." Rome is like Sodom because it is terribly wicked and immoral, and destined to be destroyed. Rome is like Egypt because, as we noted in the introduction to the seven trumpets, Rome is oppressing the people of God and imprisoning them.

11:9 **"three and a half days"**: This corresponds to the three and a half years of their preaching.

All the people from all the world are able to see their bodies; people of many lands were in Rome all the time, conducting the business of commerce and politics.

11:10-11 The celebration of the wicked Romans over the suppression of the Christian witness will be short-lived. God will "breathe life into their bodies" as God breathed life into Adam's body in Genesis 2; their message will again be proclaimed, terrifying the Romans. (Note Matt 28:4: at the moment of Jesus' resurrection, "The guards shook from fear and fell down, as though they were dead.")

11:12 "they were taken up to heaven in a cloud": This is not the event commonly referred to (in fundamentalist theology) as the rapture. It is totally consistent with the portrayal of the two witnesses as Moses and Elijah. Josephus, a Jewish historian who died a little after 100 A.D., reports the legend that Moses was taken up into heaven and hidden from his followers by a cloud. Elijah was taken up into heaven and seen no more. Likewise Jesus was taken up into heaven into a cloud. Thus, John is being completely consistent in his imagery.

The meaning of **"Come up here"** is the same as 4:1 where it meant an opening of heaven to John. Here it means that heaven is opened to receive those who have faithfully discharged their duty of preaching God's message, even unto death. To suggest that this means the Rapture is to impose from outside an interpretation which is foreign to the text.

11:13 "a tenth": This means only a small portion of Rome experienced this natural upheaval. As we have seen above, "the city" can represent the entire Empire and not just the metropolis on the Tiber.

"Seven thousand people were killed": In 1 Kings 19:18 the Lord says to Elijah, "Yet I will leave seven thousand in Israel, all the knees that have not bowed to Baal"; these were the righteous remnant, the remaining faithful ones. Here the seven thousand are killed in reparation for the deaths of the righteous witnesses to God.

"praised . . . God": Literally, they "glorified" God. In the vocabulary of all the writings attributed to John, to glorify God and to repent are synonymous. Thus the deaths of the two witnesses and their message bring about life for many Romans. John does have optimism that the message of the gospel will bring about repentance.

THINKING ALOUD

Those who take Revelation as a semi-literal, coded blueprint of the future of the human race yet to be fulfilled interpret the two witnesses as two literal individuals who will come preaching just before the great tribulation. And since the burial place of Moses is unknown and there is an ancient tradition that he was bodily assumed into heaven, and since Elijah's bodily assumption into heaven is recorded in Scripture, many of the literalists believe that it will actually be Moses and Elijah who will return to earth in our future, the whole world being able to see them due to television. (This latter point is, in logic, known as begging the question: if you cannot explain the text using the elements present in the text, add something completely foreign to the text which makes sense and proves your point.) This is patently absurd and robs Holy Scripture of its meaning for us.

The "two witnesses" are symbolized by John as Joshua and Zerubbabel, as Moses and Elijah, and as Christian witnesses who faithfully pronounced the fiery words of God's judgement on a wicked society, even to the point of falling victim to the evils of that society. It has been suggested that here are represented the preachers of the old era, Moses and Elijah; the preachers of the intertestamental era, Joshua and Zerubbabel; and the preachers of the era of John's day, reminiscent of Peter and Paul who both died in Rome because of their proclamation of the gospel.

The message of John is one of encouragement, that in every age there will be witnesses to the gospel; and though they be struck down, others will arise to take their place. The gospel will march on unhindered to the end of time.

11:14 The "third" woe will occur in 12:12 when Satan is thrown down to earth.

G. The Seventh Trumpet: Heavenly Worship (11:15-18)

The Seventh Trumpet [15]Then the seventh angel blew his trumpet. There were loud voices in heaven, saying, "The kingdom of the world now belongs to our Lord and to his Anointed, and he will reign forever and ever." [16]The twenty-four elders who sat on their thrones before God prostrated themselves and worshiped God [17]and said:

> "We give thanks to you, Lord God almighty,
> who are and who were.
> For you have assumed your great power
> and have established your reign.
> [18] The nations raged,
> but your wrath has come,
> and the time for the dead to be judged,
> and to recompense your servants, the
> prophets,
> and the holy ones and those who fear your
> name,
> the small and the great alike,
> and to destroy those who destroy the earth."

11:15 With the repentance of the people following the ascension of the witnesses the earthly realms transfer their authority to heaven. This verse, along with the "Hallelujah" from 19:2, forms the text for Handel's great "Hallelujah Chorus."

11:18 The time long awaited is now here—except that it will have to wait through the seven scenes—for the righteous to be rewarded and the wicked to receive final destruction.

Section 4: The Seven Scenes

Introduction

In this section is presented a series of scenes which begin with the birth of the Messiah and continue through the time of preparation for the judgement. This section illustrates how the writer is not following a strict time line, but jumps back and forth in time for dramatic purposes.

Thus far John has addressed the present situation of the Church (Section 1), sketched the future of the Church and the Roman Empire (Section 2, the seven seals), and described how God is warning Rome and calling it to repentance (Section 3, the seven trumpets). Now he will retrace all of salvation history from the time of the birth of the Messiah to his own birth.

It was typical of apocalyptic literature for the writer to re-tell the story of history from the time of the alleged writer (in this case, John the Apostle) to the time of the actual writer so that the reader could be placed historically within the revelation. This history was of necessity a world history, for God is the God of all nations. Chapter 12 serves this historical survey function in Revelation.

This section is the pivotal one, introducing an intensifying slide towards the destruction of Rome and culminating in a description of the final victory of God and the inauguration of the new heavens and earth.

11:19 "Then God's temple in heaven was opened": John is again being permitted to look into heaven.

"the ark of his covenant": The ark of the covenant was the gold-covered wooden chest built by Moses which contained the tablets of the Ten Commandments. The Commandments represented the covenant between God and his people. It appears for the first time here in Revelation, and represents a view into the most holy place (the "holy of holies") of heaven's temple.

The "lightning" and "thunder" and "hailstorm" are all general demonstrations of divine power and not specific events.

A. Scenes 1–3: The Story of the Woman, the Dragon, and the Child (ch. 12)

12 The Woman and the Dragon [1]A great sign appeared in the sky, a woman clothed with the sun, with the moon under her feet, and on her head a crown of twelve stars. [2]She was with child and wailed aloud in pain as she labored to give birth. [3]Then another sign appeared in the sky; it was a huge red dragon, with seven heads and ten horns, and on its heads were seven diadems. [4]Its tail swept away a third of the stars in the sky and hurled them down to the earth. Then the dragon stood before the woman about to give birth, to devour her child when she gave birth. [5]She gave birth to a son, a male child, destined to rule all the nations with an iron rod. Her child was caught up to God and his throne. ⁶The woman herself fled into the desert where she had a place prepared by God, that there she might be taken care of for twelve hundred and sixty days.

⁷Then war broke out in heaven; Michael and his angels battled against the dragon. The dragon and its angels fought back, ⁸but they did not prevail and there was no longer any place for them in heaven. ⁹The huge dragon, the ancient serpent, who is called the Devil and Satan, who deceived the whole world, was thrown down to earth, and its angels were thrown down with it.

¹⁰ Then I heard a loud voice in heaven say:
  "Now have salvation and power come,
    and the kingdom of our God
    and the authority of his Anointed.
  For the accuser of our brothers is cast out,
    who accuses them before our God day and night.
¹¹ They conquered him by the blood of the
    Lamb
    and by the word of their testimony;
    love for life did not deter them from death.
¹² Therefore, rejoice, you heavens,
    and you who dwell in them.
  But woe to you, earth and sea,
    for the Devil has come down to you in great fury,
    for he knows he has but a short time."

¹³When the dragon saw that it had been thrown down to the earth, it pursued the woman who had given birth to the male child. ¹⁴But the woman was given the two wings of the great eagle, so that she could fly to her place in the desert, where, far from the serpent, she was taken care of for a year, two years, and a half-year. ¹⁵The serpent, however, spewed a torrent of water out of his mouth after the woman to sweep her away with the current. ¹⁶But the earth helped the woman and opened its mouth and swallowed the flood that the dragon spewed out of its mouth. ¹⁷Then the dragon became angry with the woman and went off to wage war against the rest of her offspring, those who keep God's commandments and bear witness to Jesus. ¹⁸It took its position on the sand of the sea.

The key to the interpretation of this scene comes from ancient mythology. An ancient Greek myth described how the dragon Python desired to kill Apollo, the newborn son of Zeus, but was foiled when his mother, Leto, escaped to an island where Apollo was born. Apollo returned to kill the dragon in its cave. In Egypt, Set the red dragon chased Isis and was killed by her son Horus, offspring of the chief god Osiris. The background to these myths is the primal story of the dragon of darkness who desires to kill the sun god, son of the chief of gods, at the moment of his birth, but instead is killed by him at the dawning of the new day.

John sees in this ancient story a parallel to the story of how Mary/Israel gave birth to the Son of God, Jesus; the attack of Satan, that ancient serpent, in Rome's persecutions of Israel the Church (paralleled by the slaughter of the holy innocents); and the archangel Michael's expulsion of the dragon Satan as a result of its defeat by Christ through his obedient death on the cross. John uses the story as a backdrop to recount the story of Christ and his Church up to John's time.

Comparison of the Egyptian and Greek myths with Revelation

Character:	Egyptian Myth	Greek Myth	Revelation
The Chief God	Osiris	Zeus	God
His son, god of the sun	Horus	Apollo	Jesus
Mother of the newborn god	Isis	Leto	Mary/Israel
The Dragon	A red dragon	Python	Satan

12:1   In this scene the identity of the "woman" shifts from earthly Israel to spiritual Israel. In addition, since the woman gives birth to Christ, the Blessed Virgin Mary is often portrayed using descriptions from these verses.

"whose clothes were the sun": This is drawn from the primal myth referred to above—she shines with divine radiance.

"moon was under her feet": Israel's whole system of festivals and worship was based on a lunar calendar.

"a crown made of twelve stars was on her head": This represents the kingdom of the twelve tribes of Israel.

12:3 **"red dragon"**: The dragon in the ancient myth was red, the color of blood. Jeremiah referred to the invading Babylonain king Nebuchadnezzar as a dragon (Jer 51:34), and Ezekiel pictured Pharaoh as a dragon as well (Ezek 29:3).

"seven heads . . . a crown on each head": At this point the images are purely symbolic: seven heads, each with a crown, represents complete power to rule on earth. The many heads also symbolize dynastic power: Satan works through the Roman Empire.

"ten horns": Ten symbolizes completeness, horns symbolize power; therefore, on earth the dragon/Empire/Satan appears to exercise total power over its kingdom.

12:4 "swept away a third of the stars in the sky": In Daniel there is a ram with a horn which drags down stars from the sky (Dan 8:10). The stars were considered to be angelic representatives of the nations; this represents Satan's conquering of the nations through evil empires like Rome.

"Then the dragon turned toward the woman": As in the ancient myth, Satan turns on the woman to kill her son. The powers of evil sought through the slaughter of the holy innocents and again in the crucifixion to be rid of the obedient Son of God.

12:5 "a son . . . destined to rule all the nations with an iron rod": This quotation of 2:27 (which in turn is quoting Psalm 2) reveals that the son is Christ.

"caught up to God and his throne": Through the resurrection and ascension Christ triumphed over Satan's efforts.

12:6 "The woman herself fled into the desert": This is the desert of the Exodus. Though in the Bible the desert is usually a place of chaos and testing (as in the journey of Elijah and the temptations of Jesus), for the Israelites the desert was a place of sustenance where God provided them with bread from heaven. The woman who was Israel is now spiritual Israel, the Church.

"there she might be taken care of for twelve hundred and sixty days": This is Daniel's three and a half years of ordeal. John refers to this three-and-a-half-year period in three ways in the following contexts:

1,260 days	the two witnesses have power to prophesy (11:3)
	the woman is cared for in the desert (12:6)
42 months	the nations will trample the holy city (11:2)
	the beast from the sea is given authority (13:5)

a year, two years, and a half-year
the woman is cared for in the desert (12:14)

12:7 "Then war broke out in heaven; Michael and his angles battled against the dragon": From Daniel 10:13 John draws the figure of Michael, whose name means "mighty one of God," and describes his defeat of Satan. This defeat occurred that dark day when the Son of God, human representative of all humankind, in a single act of obedience on behalf of all humankind, died upon the cross. On that day God's mighty one, Michael, evicted the slanderer—the accuser—and all his confreres from the heavenly realms.

12:9 "the ancient serpent": This refers to the serpent in the garden of Eden which, beginning about one hundred years before Christ, had been identified with Satan.
"the Devil": This descriptive name for the opponent means "slanderer."
"Satan" means "accuser" and refers to the earlier Jewish conception that Satan was a heavenly being in God's court who served the function of a prosecuting attorney. It was when he began to overstep his bounds that he began to be called the slanderer who falsely accuses the people of God.

12:10-12 Again heaven breaks forth in song at the victory over Satan.

12:11 How did the Church win the victory over the Evil One? First, because of the obedient death of Christ, whose "blood" was shed like that of a sacrificial "Lamb"; and second, because it was faithful in proclaiming the "word of their testimony" to the point that "love for life did not deter them from death." This timeless recipe for spiritual victory is as valid today as in 95 A.D.

12:13 Here "the woman" is spiritual Israel, the Church, whom the Devil will seek to trouble because of his defeat.

12:14 "two wings . . . like those of an eagle": Reinforcing the link with the Exodus is this image from Exodus 19:4: "You have seen for yourselves how I treated the Egyptians, and how I bore you up on eagle wings and brought you here to myself." The place where God brought them to himself was Sinai, in the "desert."

"a year, two years, and a half-year": Here for the only time in the book John repeats the exact wording of Daniel, cementing the link. Yet again we are told, the repetition serving as reassurance to the reader, that God will care for his people for as long as the ordeal lasts.

12:15 "The serpent . . . spewed a torrent of water out of his mouth after the woman to sweep her away": The dragon/enemy of God's people is referred to as a water dragon in various places in the Old Testament (e.g., Ezek 29:3). Since his home is the primeval abyss which contains the waters under the earth, water would be a natural weapon for him. Perhaps John has in mind the time Pharaoh tried to drown the Hebrew babies in the Nile, which corresponds to the slaughter of the Holy Innocents in the New Testament.

12:16 "the earth . . . swallowed the flood": Perhaps this refers to Numbers 16:33 when the earth swallowed the unrighteous Israelites in order to protect the holiness of the others.

12:17 "the rest of her offspring": If Satan cannot defeat Christ or his Church as a whole, he will attack individual Christians.

12:18 This verse is transitional to the next scene. The Romans often attacked from the sea. The dragon, the power behind Rome, is poised there.

THINKING ALOUD

A stained glass window in Grace-St. Luke's Episcopal Church, Memphis, Tennessee, portrays St. Michael and the angels vanquishing the dragon. At the bottom of the picture, separated from the heavenly scene by clouds, is a bombed-out battlefield complete with Patton tanks and B-17 aircraft flying overhead.

The expulsion of Satan from heaven has been interpreted as applying to many different events in history, but perhaps that window in Memphis holds the key. This is not because

Satan's eviction took place during World War II; that window holds the key because of the window next to it. The other window shows in one panel Christ crucified, hands uplifted on the cross. The other panel shows Christ in exactly the same posture, but robed in kingly majesty, the peoples of the earth about his feet, a rainbow around him.

Satan's expulsion took place on Good Friday. Ever since that day the evil One has pursued the Church throughout the world, and each time evil is overcome by good, Satan's defeat is made more real.

B. Scene 4: The Beast from the Sea (13:1-10)

13   The First Beast   ¹Then I saw a beast come out of the sea with ten horns and seven heads; on its horns were ten diadems, and on its heads blasphemous name[s]. ²The beast I saw was like a leopard, but it had feet like a bear's, and its mouth was like the mouth of a lion. To it the dragon gave its own power and throne, along with great authority. ³I saw that one of its heads seemed to have been mortally wounded, but this mortal wound was healed. Fascinated, the whole world followed after the beast. ⁴They worshiped the dragon because it gave its authority to the beast; they also worshiped the beast and said, "Who can compare with the beast or who can fight against it?"

⁵The beast was given a mouth uttering proud boasts and blasphemies, and it was given authority to act for forty-two months. ⁶It opened its mouth to utter blasphemies against God, blaspheming his name and his dwelling and those who dwell in heaven. ⁷It was also allowed to wage war against the holy ones and conquer them, and it was granted authority over every tribe, people, tongue, and nation. ⁸All the inhabitants of the earth will worship it, all whose names were not written from the foundation of the world in the book of life, which belongs to the Lamb who was slain.

⁹ Whoever has ears ought to hear these words.
¹⁰ Anyone destined for captivity goes into captivity.
    Anyone destined to be slain by the sword
        shall be slain by the sword.
Such is the faithful endurance of the holy ones.

13:1   This beast looks like Satan because it is in his image. It "comes up out of the sea." When John looked from Patmos in the direction of Rome he saw the sea. The Romans frequently arrived from the sea when invading a country. The sea is the abode of the dragon, and so the dragon's realm is the place from which the Roman Empire comes.

Here the **"seven heads"** each with a **"blasphemous name"** represents the seven emperors since B.C. 27, the end of the Republic: Augustus, Tiberius, Caligula, Claudius, Nero, Vespasian, and Titus. During 68–69 A.D. there really was no one emperor; instead, three generals, Galba, Otho, and Vitellius, succeeded each other briefly on the throne. If we count them we have ten, which may be signified by the "ten horns.'" Or, the ten horns (as we saw above) may represent complete power to rule. So, this beast represents imperial Rome.

13:2 Drawing from the beast in Daniel 7:3-7, Rome is described as an accumulation of previous empires:

leopard	Persia
bear	Media (not the Soviet Union!)
lion	Babylon

John makes it clear where the Roman Empire gets its "great authority"—from Satan.

13:3 **"one of its heads seemed to have been mortally wounded"**: This is a reference to the Nero Redivivus ("Nero revived") myth, a story going around the Empire at the time of John that Nero had not really committed suicide after being arrested and thrown into prison for crimes against the state. This story was taken very seriously, as three pretenders claiming to be Nero Redivivus appeared between 69 and 88 A.D.

13:5 Here we have a clear reference to the Roman emperor's claim to divinity which lead him to persecute the Christians for forty-two months (again, Daniel's three and a half years).

13:6-7 Here is a true picture of one who is against—anti—Christ. The last part of verse 7 mirrors the words spoken about Christ in the opening vision of Revelation, but here they are about a diabolical emperor, an antichrist.

13:8 This verse seems to suggest some kind of predestination, but it is entirely consistent with Ephesians 1:4: "as he chose us in him, before the foundation of the world, to be holy

and without blemish before him." This is not so much a reference to a predetermining foresight of God as it is a hindsight
on the part of the author, a retrospection that can see the hand
of God at work from before time, something that could not
be seen until this moment of spiritual enlightenment. (How
often on a road trip have you turned around to see where you
have been and seen a vista which you completely missed until
you had already gone through it?) From before time God was
planning to call and to save the people whom he would create.

**"in the book of life, which belongs to the Lamb who was
slain"**: As we saw above in the comment on 3:5, ancient Persian cities had tax rolls, and to be recorded therein meant
citizenship in the city. The "book of life" is the citizenship
roll book of the heavenly Jerusalem and is kept by Christ, the
"Lamb who was slain."

13:9 This refrain was repeated at the end of each of the
seven letters, and was used by Christ in the Gospels as well.
There it was addressed to Christians, as it is here.

13:10 This is a reference to Jeremiah 43:10-11:

> Thus says the LORD of hosts, the God of Israel: I will send
> for my servant Nebuchadnezzar, king of Babylon, and bring
> him here. . . . He shall come and strike the land of Egypt:
> with death, whoever is marked for death;
> with exile, everyone destined for exile;
> with the sword, all who are intended for the sword.

This verse seems quite fatalistic, but John is citing a prophecy
concerning the ruler of ancient Babylon in order to describe
the ruler of this Roman Babylon, trying to get his people to
look matter-of-factly at the challenge that faces them, encouraging them to "faithful endurance."

C. Scene 5: The Beast from the Land (13:11-18)

The Second Beast ¹¹Then I saw another beast come up out
of the earth; it had two horns like a lamb's but spoke like
a dragon. ¹²It wielded all the authority of the first beast in
its sight and made the earth and its inhabitants worship the

first beast, whose mortal wound had been healed. ¹³It performed great signs, even making fire come down from heaven to earth in the sight of everyone. ¹⁴It deceived the inhabitants of the earth with the signs it was allowed to perform in the sight of the first beast, telling them to make an image for the beast who had been wounded by the sword and revived. ¹⁵It was then permitted to breathe life into the beast's image, so that the beast's image could speak and [could] have anyone who did not worship it put to death. ¹⁶It forced all the people, small and great, rich and poor, free and slave, to be given a stamped image on their right hands or their foreheads, ¹⁷so that no one could buy or sell except one who had the stamped image of the beast's name or the number that stood for its name.

¹⁸Wisdom is needed here; one who understands can calculate the number of the beast, for it is a number that stands for a person. His number is six hundred and sixty-six.

As we analyze the description of this beast we shall see that it represents the emperor worship cult established by Domitian in the eastern provinces of the Empire.

13:11 **"out of the earth"**: According to ancient, apocalyptic tradition, there are two primordial beasts, one from the sea and one from the land. This beast is the companion of the first.

"two horns like a lamb's but spoke like a dragon": This beast is a diabolical, deceptive imitation of the Lamb; it tries to imitate the worship of the true God, but in reality its devilish voice entices people to worship the demonic. This is the original dragon in sheep's clothing.

13:12 **"It wielded all the authority of the first beast . . . whose mortal wound had been healed"**: This is another reference to Domitian as another Nero, who committed suicide by stabbing himself in the throat, but who was commonly believed still to be alive (the Nero Redivivus myth).

The emperor worship cult was in Domitian's employ, and this second beast forced everyone "to worship the first beast," that is, Domitian.

13:14 The emperor worship cult possessed no real spiritual power, but had to try to trick people with sham "signs" made to look like they had been performed in the power of their divine emperor Domitian.

13:15 "the beast's image could speak": In the ancient world it was commonly believed that statues of a god communicated its power to its worshippers. Trickery of all sorts involving the statues of gods was common, an example being found in the deuterocanonical book Daniel, Bel, and the Dragon, where Daniel proves that the Babylonian idol Bel isn't really eating the food offered to it.

The largest statue of Domitian ever discovered in Asia Minor was excavated in Ephesus, John's home city. It is sixteen feet tall and hollow, allowing an imperial priest to hide within it and make it appear to talk (something that would have been believable in that superstitious age). Archaeology has thus not only provided a historical reference within the Book of Revelation, but also serves as evidence that the book is indeed referring to the reign of Domitian.

13:16 The original Greek has a poetic, almost dirge-like sound to it:

"It forced all the people,
        small and great,
            rich and poor,
                free and slave,
to be given a stamped image on their right hands or their foreheads. . . ."

The Greek word for "image" or "mark" is a technical term used to describe the emperor's seal on official documents. Our equivalent would be something like the president's signature on a bill, or a notary public's seal. Slaves were branded on the forehead, and those who worship the emperor are his slaves.

We are not to use this verse to try to identify some universal mark (such as the Social Security number, or a tattoo visible only under ultraviolet light, or the universal bar code pricing system, as some imaginative persons have suggested) which is specifically the mark of the Antichrist. It is a figurative mark.

In addition, this marking of the beast is a grotesque, bizarre imitation of God's marking of his people described in chapter

7. The marking on the foreheads by God is a gracious mark of protection.

The fact that John included "their right hands" is a clear reference to the Jewish phylacteries, small leather boxes containing Holy Scripture verses, which were tied to the forehead and right forearm by means of leather straps. These were considered a devotion to God and a protection from evil. The beast perverts all that is holy and adapts it to his own use.

With the emergence of this beast we have completed what some have called "the Unholy Trinity." The dragon (Satan) is the father of all lies, and gives his authority to the first beast. The first beast, from the sea, is a parody of Christ: he tries to look like a lamb (but without the wounds of the sacrificial lamb!), and he was given authority, as was Christ, over people of every tribe, nation, language, and race. The second beast, from the land, parodies the Holy Spirit: he works miracles, puts breath into the idol (the Greek word for "breath" is *pneuma*, which also means "Spirit"), and leads in worship of the first beast.

13:17 **"no one could buy or sell":** The Greek word for "image" also described the emperor's image on coins, thus explaining why they couldn't buy or sell anything without the mark. John tells us that this "image" stands for "the beast's name or the number that stood for its name."

13:18 With "wisdom" one can "calculate" the meaning of the "number of the beast," which is "a number that stands for a person."

Centuries of often fantastic speculation have gone into the discernment of the meaning of this number. One of the latest has to do with a former president who has six letters in each of his three names, Ronald Wilson Reagan. All of this speculation is unnecessary.

Suffice it to say here that there was a Jewish study of words and numbers, which arose from the fact that Hebrew letters also served as numerals. We have already been told that the beast resembled Nero Redivivus. If we take the Greek name of Neron Kaisar (Nero Caesar), spell it in Hebrew NRON KSR, and add up the numerical values of these Hebrew letter/numerals, we get 666. By adopting the interpretation ''Neron Kaisar'' we get an answer totally consistent with everything else we've seen in Revelation thus far. (A full discussion of this appears in the appendix to this book.)

THINKING ALOUD

In chapter 13 we see portrayed the evil that is perpetrated when political power makes use of religion to validate itself and coerce its subjects. We have seen this story play itself out over and over in history. The founding fathers of the United States, having recently fought a war to become free from a similar tyranny of church and state, forbad in the Constitution the establishment of religion by Congress, or the inhibition by Congress of the free exercise of religion, seeking to avoid this unholy wedding between religion and politics.

However, this has not kept the two apart even in the United States. Politicians again and again appeal to religious and moral principles to justify political actions. We should not wish political actions to be contrary to those principles; but for politicians to seek to justify themselves in controversial matters primarily by an appeal to religion and morals is to risk calling forth once again the beasts from the sea and from the land.

D. Scene 6: The Lamb and His Followers (14:1-5)

14 The Lamb's Companions ¹Then I looked and there was the Lamb standing on Mount Zion, and with him a hundred and forty-four thousand who had his name and his Father's name written on their foreheads. ²I heard a sound from heaven like the sound of rushing water or a loud peal of thunder. The sound I heard was like that of harpists playing their harps. ³They were singing [what seemed to be] a new hymn before the throne, before the four living creatures and the elders. No one could learn this hymn except the hundred and forty-four thousand who had been ransomed from the earth. ⁴These are they who were not defiled with women; they are virgins and these are the ones who follow the Lamb wherever he goes. They have been ransomed as the first-fruits of the human race for God and the Lamb. ⁵On their lips no deceit has been found; they are unblemished.

14:1 "**Mount Zion**" is the name of the hill upon which the Temple in Jerusalem was built. References to the Temple have consistently been referring to God's heavenly habitation. The Mount Zion referred to here is also the heavenly one as evidenced by 14:3 which refers to God's throne, the four living creatures, and the twenty-four elders.

"**a hundred and forty-four thousand**": This is the same group as in chapter 7. In contrast to those bearing the mark of the beast, they "had his [Christ the Lamb's] name and his Father's name written on their foreheads."

14:2 Whereas the voice of God and of Christ has been compared to "rushing water or a loud peal of thunder," it also sounds like "harpists playing on their harps." According to 1 Kings 10:12 Solomon made lyres and harps for the singers in the Temple; these were standard musical instruments for the earthly Temple.

14:3 Here again is the "new hymn" which we saw in 5:9. This song belongs only to the redeemed; it cannot be sung except by them. This has given rise to the poetic notion that the saints sing the song of redemption which angels cannot sing.

14:4 "**virgins**": John is using the Old Testament metaphor in which the prophets referred to Israel as an "adulteress" when it fell into idolatry, an allusion which we saw in 2:20-22. Thus John means that these are the saints, specifically, those who abstained from emperor worship.

"**who follow the Lamb wherever he goes**": This is the very Johannine picture of Christ the Good Shepherd which we see in John 10 and Revelation 7:17. They follow their shepherd even to death.

"**ransomed**": Death delivered them from the ordeal.

"**the firstfruits of the human race**": This is a reference to the Law of Moses in which the first portion of the harvest is to be given to God. James 1:18 says, "He willed to give us birth by the word of truth that we may be a kind of firstfruits of his creatures." This is not a reference to the order in which these 144,000 reached heaven (i.e., before anyone else). It is an indication of their status.

14:5 Zephaniah 3:13 speaks of the remnant of Israel in this way: "They shall do no wrong and speak no lies; Nor shall there be found in their mouths a deceitful tongue." This also recalls the innocence of the Suffering Servant of God in Isaiah 53:9, which says that he had not "spoken any falsehood."

E. Interlude: The Three Angels (14:6-13)

The Three Angels ⁶Then I saw another angel flying high overhead, with everlasting good news to announce to those who dwell on earth, to every nation, tribe, tongue, and people. ⁷He said in a loud voice, "Fear God and give him glory, for his time has come to sit in judgment. Worship him who made heaven and earth and sea and springs of water."

⁸ A second angel followed, saying:
"Fallen, fallen is Babylon the great,
    that made all the nations drink
    the wine of her licentious passion."

⁹A third angel followed them and said in a loud voice, "Anyone who worships the beast or its image, or accepts its mark on forehead or hand, ¹⁰will also drink the wine of God's fury, poured full strength into the cup of his wrath, and will be tormented in burning sulfur before the holy angels and before the Lamb. ¹¹The smoke of the fire that torments them will rise forever and ever, and there will be no relief day or night for those who worship the beast or its image or accept the mark of its name." ¹²Here is what sustains the holy ones who keep God's commandments and their faith in Jesus.

¹³I heard a voice from heaven say, "Write this: Blessed are the dead who die in the Lord from now on." "Yes," said the Spirit, "let them find rest from their labors, for their works accompany them."

14:6-7 Although we have had several previews of God's judgement against the wicked, this "angel" tells us that we are to kneel before God because "[God's] time has come to sit in judgement." The angel's "good news" is for the suffering Christians, as well as being a final proclamation calling for the repentance of the wicked.

14:8 "**Babylon**" was the capital of the ancient empire which invaded Jerusalem and destroyed the Temple in B.C. 587.

It is a fitting name for conquering Rome, which exported its idolatry and paganism and thus infected the entire western world with its immorality.

The "second angel" proclaims that Babylon has fallen using words taken from Isaiah 21:9b: "Fallen, fallen is Babylon, / And all the images of her gods are smashed to the ground."

14:9 The "third angel" proclaims a final warning to all participants in the emperor worship cult.

14:10 **"drink the wine of God's fury, poured full strength into the cup of his wrath":** Notice the following passages from the Old and New Testaments:

> Psalm 75:9: "Yes, a cup is in the LORD's hand, foaming wine, fully spiced."

> Isaiah 51:17: "You who drank at the LORD's hand the cup of his wrath; / Who drained to the dregs the bowl of staggering!"

> Jeremiah 25:15-16 "For thus said the LORD, the God of Israel, to me: Take this cup of foaming wine from my hand, and have all the nations to whom I will send you drink it. They shall drink, and be convulsed, and go mad, because of the sword I will send among them."

> Luke 22:42 "Father, if you are willing, take this cup away from me; still, not my will but yours be done."

Here is a recurring Old Testament image of the cup of God's wrath against sinners. Christ received this cup representatively for all humankind upon the cross. Now, those who did not accept the Lamb as their sacrifice must drink the cup themselves. To drink it "full strength" means that it is undiluted (wine was usually heavily diluted with water in those days).

"tormented in burning sulphur": Notice Isaiah 34:8-10, where the prophet describes the fate of sinful Edom. Verse 10 says, "Night and day it shall not be quenched, its smoke shall rise forever." We first see fire and brimstone in the Bible at the destruction of Sodom and Gomorrah, and we saw it in Revelation 9:14 where it described the attacking cavalry.

14:11-12 A clear warning to those yet unrepentant, set against a clear exhortation to the Church.

14:13   This is a message of comfort to those yet enduring the great ordeal. The command "write this" is an indication of the certainty of the blessing.

THINKING ALOUD

It is difficult for us today to imagine the feelings of the Christians going through Domitian's persecutions, so it is difficult for us to deal with verses such as 14:10 above. If indeed Revelation inherits the tradition of John the Apostle, recall that the nickname of John and his brother James was "sons of thunder." This is because, in their quick-temperedness, James and John wanted to call down fire from heaven on a Samaritan village which refused hospitality to Jesus and his disciples.

Rather than trying to judge such people in the Church today, with their harsh view of God's justice (for it would be inappropriate for us to judge them), let us instead examine our own understanding of God's justice in the light of the gospel, and recall that with what judgement we judge, we shall be judged.

F. Scene 7: The Harvesting of the Earth (14:14-20)

The Harvest of the Earth   14Then I looked and there was a white cloud, and sitting on the cloud one who looked like a son of man, with a gold crown on his head and a sharp sickle in his hand. 15Another angel came out of the temple, crying out in a loud voice to the one sitting on the cloud, "Use your sickle and reap the harvest, for the time to reap has come, because the earth's harvest is fully ripe." 16So the one who was sitting on the cloud swung his sickle over the earth, and the earth was harvested.

17Then another angel came out of the temple in heaven who also had a sharp sickle. 18Then another angel [came] from the altar, [who] was in charge of the fire, and cried out in a loud voice to the one who had the sharp sickle, "Use your sharp sickle and cut the clusters from the earth's vines, for its grapes are ripe." 19So the angel swung his sickle over the earth and cut the earth's vintage. He threw it into the great wine press of God's fury. 20The wine press was trodden outside the city and blood poured out of the wine press to the height of a horse's bridle for two hundred miles.

Verses 14-20 introduce the execution of God's judgement, depicted as the pouring out of seven bowls of his anger, by describing it in terms of a grape harvest.

14:14 Here Christ is described in images by now familiar in Revelation, drawn from Daniel 7. The "gold crown" is not merely a crown but a wreath. The wreath of thorns which the Savior endured is now a golden garland which shows forth his glory, a gold wreath like the ones we see on the statues of the Caesars, the wreath of victory like the laurel wreaths given athletes. He holds a sickle and is ready for the harvest.

14:15 **"Use your sickle and reap the harvest . . . because the earth's harvest is fully ripe":** Compare what the angel says to Joel 4:13: "Apply the sickle for the harvest is ripe; / Come and tread, for the wine press is full; / The vats overflow, for great is their malice."

14:17-19 The swinging of the sickle by the Son of Man is the signal for the workers, the angels, to begin the harvest (not unlike the President throwing out the first ball).

14:20 **"two hundred miles":** In the Greek this is sixteen hundred stadia. The number may be symbolic of the entire world: the four winds times the four corners of the earth times one hundred equals sixteen hundred.

"to the height of a horse's bridle": The non-biblical apocalypse 1 Enoch 100:3 says, "And the horses shall walk up to the breast in the blood of sinners, And the chariot shall be submerged to its height." We also find this wording in the Talmud, an ancient Jewish commentary on the Law of Moses, where it describes the bloodshed in a battle which took place at the time of the emperor Hadrian. Battle is used as an image of the terrible and swift judgement of God, and is compared to the pressing of grapes, whose juice is called "the blood of the grape" in Ecclesiasticus. This is probably a preview of the battle in 19:19-21, especially since 19:15 says that in order to show God's power Christ will "tread out in the wine press the wine of the fury and wrath of God the almighty."

The imagery of these verses is used in the first verse of the famous poem written by Juliet Ward Howe in the midst of the American Civil War:

> Mine eyes have seen the glory of the coming of the Lord;
> He is trampling out the vintage where the grapes of wrath
>   are stored.
> He hath loosed the fateful lightning of his terrible swift
>   sword.
> His truth is marching on.

THINKING ALOUD

This graphic depiction of God's judgement on earth compares it to a grape harvest, the grape juice reminding John of blood. It is scenes like this, combined with the author's extremely heavy dependence on Old Testament books and texts, which make Revelation seem more like an Old Testament book, except that Christ is in it. How would the Jesus of Luke's Gospel respond to the Book of Revelation?

Section 5: The Seven Bowls of God's Anger

Introduction (15:1–16:1)

15 The Seven Last Plagues ¹Then I saw in heaven another sign, great and awe-inspiring: seven angels with the seven last plagues, for through them God's fury is accomplished.

²Then I saw something like a sea of glass mingled with fire. On the sea of glass were standing those who had won the victory over the beast and its image and the number that signified its name. They were holding God's harps, ³and they sang the song of Moses, the servant of God, and the song of the Lamb:

> "Great and wonderful are your works,
>   Lord God almighty.
> Just and true are your ways,
>   O king of the nations.
> ⁴ Who will not fear you, Lord,
>   or glorify your name?
> For you alone are holy.
>   All the nations will come
>   and worship before you,
>   for your righteous acts have been
>   revealed."

⁵After this I had another vision. The temple that is the heavenly tent of testimony opened, ⁶and the seven angels with the seven plagues came out of the temple. They were dressed in clean white linen, with a gold sash around their chests. ⁷One of the four living creatures gave the seven angels seven gold bowls filled with the fury of God, who lives forever and ever. ⁸Then the temple became so filled with the smoke from God's glory and might that no one could enter it until the seven plagues of the seven angels had been accomplished.

16 The Seven Bowls ¹I heard a loud voice speaking from the temple to the seven angels, "Go and pour out the seven bowls of God's fury upon the earth."

15:1 Here the bowls of God's anger are introduced, which will finally expend God's wrath. These seven bowls parallel quite closely the seven trumpets. However, whereas with the trumpets the destruction was only partial because it was a warning, here it is total because it is judgement.

15:2 "a sea of glass mingled with fire": In 4:6 we saw that the glass sea was the dome of heaven and the waters above the dome as described in Genesis 1. Here this same sea is mixed with fire, like a blazing red sky at sunset, or like the sky when it is lit with ripples of lightning. This symbolizes the readiness of God to execute judgement.

"the ones who had overcome": These are all the martyrs (symbolized as the 144,000), those who passed through the ordeal and are now safe in heaven, standing upon the dome of the sky with their harps to sing the praise of God. No doubt this verse has contributed to the popular depiction of saints and angels in heaven playing harps.

15:3 "they sang the song of Moses, the servant of God": There are two songs that Moses sang. One is in Exodus 15, in which Moses and the Israelites praise God for delivering them from the Egyptians through the Red Sea. While the theme of that song applies here, its content is not so much like the content of the song John quotes here as is the song of Moses in Deuteronomy 32:3-4. It describes the greatness of God and the justice of his works.

"and the song of the Lamb": The song of Moses was the old song of redemption; the song of the Lamb is the "new song" mentioned in 5:9 and 14:3.

15:5-6 Here heaven's temple is specifically referred to as "the heavenly tent of testimony," like the one Moses built for the children of Israel in the desert. Now the tent opens to allow the "seven angels" to come out from God's presence. Their "clean white linen" robes and "gold sash around their chest" reflect the apparel of Christ in chapter 1 and that of the priests in the Old Testament. On earth God is served by human priests, in heaven, angelic ones.

15:7 One of the cherubim, the "four living creatures," the highest order of the angelic host, hands out the bowls. In Ezekiel 10:7 it is a cherub that takes fire from the altar of God in heaven and gives it to one dressed in linen who took it out.

15:8 "filled with . . . smoke": When Moses finished setting up the original sacred tent it was filled with the glory of God, and Moses was not able to enter the tent for the cloud of glory. Similarly, when the first permanent Temple was dedicated by Solomon, it was filled with a cloud such that the priests could not enter. Also, the heavenly temple was filled with smoke in Isaiah's vision (6:4). Thus, smoke or a cloud is a sign of the presence of God in power and glory.

> ²The first angel went and poured out his bowl on the earth. Festering and ugly sores broke out on those who had the mark of the beast or worshiped its image.
>
> ³The second angel poured out his bowl on the sea. The sea turned to blood like that from a corpse; every creature living in the sea died.
>
> ⁴The third angel poured out his bowl on the rivers and springs of water. These also turned to blood. ⁵Then I heard the angel in charge of the waters say:
>
> > "You are just, O Holy One,
> >   who are and who were,
> >   in passing this sentence.
> > ⁶ For they have shed the blood of the holy ones
> >   and the prophets,

and you [have] given them blood to drink;
it is what they deserve.''
7 Then I heard the altar cry out,
''Yes, Lord God almighty,
your judgments are true and just.''

8The fourth angel poured out his bowl on the sun. It was given the power to burn people with fire. 9People were burned by the scorching heat and blasphemed the name of God who had power over these plagues, but they did not repent or give him glory.

10The fifth angel poured out his bowl on the throne of the beast. Its kingdom was plunged into darkness, and people bit their tongues in pain 11and blasphemed the God of heaven because of their pains and sores. But they did not repent of their works.

12The sixth angel emptied his bowl on the great river Euphrates. Its water was dried up to prepare the way for the kings of the East. 13I saw three unclean spirits like frogs come from the mouth of the dragon, from the mouth of the beast, and from the mouth of the false prophet. 14These were demonic spirits who performed signs. They went out to the kings of the whole world to assemble them for the battle on the great day of God the almighty. 15(''Behold, I am coming like a thief.'' Blessed is the one who watches and keeps his clothes ready, so that he may not go naked and people see him exposed.) 16They then assembled the kings in the place that is named Armageddon in Hebrew.

17The seventh angel poured out his bowl into the air. A loud voice came out of the temple from the throne, saying, ''It is done.'' 18Then there were lightning flashes, rumblings, and peals of thunder, and a great earthquake. It was such a violent earthquake that there has never been one like it since the human race began on earth. 19The great city was split into three parts, and the gentile cities fell. But God remembered great Babylon, giving it the cup filled with the wine of his fury and wrath. 20Every island fled, and mountains disappeared. 21Large hailstones like huge weights came down from the sky on people, and they blasphemed God for the plague of hail because this plague was so severe.

A. The First Bowl (16:2)

The outbreak of "festering and painful sores" parallels the plague of boils in Egypt.

B. The Second Bowl (16:3)

With the second trumpet a third of the sea turned to blood. Here the entire sea turns not just to blood, but to the black, coagulated blood "from a corpse."

C. The Third Bowl (16:4-7)

16:4 Paralleling the third trumpet, here all the fresh water turns to blood as it did in Egypt.

16:6 "So you give them blood to drink, as they deserve": The idea of retribution is unmistakably present here. To drink blood was one of the most abominable sins in Judaism, and the Jerusalem Council in the Acts of the Apostles told Christians to abstain from meat with the blood in it. Isaiah 49:26 says, "I will make your oppressors eat their own flesh, and they shall be drunk with their own blood as with the juice of the grape. All mankind shall know that I the LORD am your Savior." Ezekiel 38:21 describes the day of judgement as a time in which "every man's sword [will be] against his brother." Thus the time of upheaval and judgement will be a time of internal strife, division, and civil war.

The song in 5-7 parallels that above in 15:3-4.

D. The Fourth Bowl (16:8-9)

Whereas the fourth trumpet caused the sun to dim, here it heats up to the point that it scorches people. No one is spared, and no one turns to God (repents) and praises him. The fact that John mentions that no one repents suggests that they could have done so even in the midst of the execution of judgement.

E. The Fifth Bowl (16:10-11)

This bowl is poured directly over Rome and results in a painful darkness like that in the plagues of Egypt. Again, this does not lead to repentance. (This may allude to the eruption of Vesuvius in 72 A.D., which destroyed Pompeii.)

F. The Sixth Bowl (16:12-14)

16:12 **"The great river Euphrates . . . dried up to prepare the way"**: In Jeremiah 50:38 the punitive invasion of Babylon is preceded by a drying up of her waters. This was fulfilled in B.C. 530 when the Persian king Cyrus diverted the Euphrates River which flowed down the middle of Babylon, marching his troops down the dry river bed and into the city from its unprotected side. Thus, the one barrier to invasion which the Babylonians probably felt they would never have to worry about was overcome and their city fell. Rome, John's Babylon, cannot trust even its most sure defence when it is God Almighty who is pouring out his wrath upon her.

"a way for the kings of the East": This is a reference to the Parthians and other barbaric tribes to the east of the Roman Empire.

16:13 **"three unclean spirits like frogs"**: Here John's descriptions become even more grotesque. The Zoroastrian religion, the religion of ancient Persia, gave us (through the Judaism of the Exile) the concept of dualism (light versus darkness, good versus evil, which John and the other apocalyptic writers subscribed to very thoroughly), including angels and demons. In Zoroastrianism frogs were considered to be the source of plagues and of death.

There are three frogs here, one from the mouth of each of the unholy trinity—the dragon (Satan), the beast (Domitian), and the false prophet (the emperor worship cult). This calls to mind 1 Kings 22:22 which speaks of a lying spirit which will proceed from the mouths of the false prophets.

16:14 These lying frogs went forth from Satan and the Roman emperor in order to deceive the rulers of the Empire's member nations and to summon them to gather ''for the battle on the great day of God the almighty." Their efforts are futile, for that is to be the day of God's great victory. This recalls the idea seen before (6:17) of the day of God's wrath, and the day of God foreseen in 2 Peter 3:12.

16:15   "Behold, I am coming like a thief!": In Matthew 24:43 Jesus, in a parable about readiness, says that if the owner of the house had known at what time the thief were coming he would have been watching and would not have let his house be broken into. In Revelation 3:3 he told the sleepy church of Sardis to keep awake, else he would come like a thief at a time unknown to them.

"so that he may not go naked and people see him exposed": In Mark 13:16 Jesus tells his disciples that if, on the day of the Abomination of Desolation (which recalls the day described in Daniel when Antiochus set up the statue of Zeus in the Temple), they are caught out in the field, they are not to go back for their coat. Christ had scolded the Laodiceans for thinking that they were rich when they were really naked (3:17).

John is foretelling the judgement of Rome to his readers, and he interrupts the vision of that judgement with the voice of Christ, reminding his readers that, if they remain vigilant and ready, they will not be caught unprepared.

16:16   Picking up the thought in verse 14 before the interlude, the armies called by the emperor will gather at "Armageddon." Volumes could be written about events that took place at the Hill of Megiddo, the literal meaning of Har Megiddon. Among others: in the Book of Judges a battle of cosmic proportions took place there; in 2 Kings, King Ahaziah of Judah died there in battle; Pharaoh Nico of Egypt killed King Josiah of Judah in battle there; Napoleon fought there; Eisenhower called it the classic battlefield. What better place in all the Roman Empire, in addressing a Christian audience familiar with the Old Testament, to place the final battle?

G. The Seventh Bowl (16:17-21)

16:17   "It is done": This recalls the cry from Jesus just before his death on the cross. It is a cry of fulfillment and completion.

16:18-19 In this judgement upon the air, a spectacular, destructive display of divine power takes place, including an earthquake so violent that "there has never been one like it since the human race began." Note Daniel 12:1, describing the time of great ordeal: "It shall be a time unsurpassed in distress since nations began until that time."

"The great city was split into three parts": That is, it was completely destroyed, and with it "the gentile cities fell" (as before, the great city is Rome).

On the expression "the cup filled with the wine of his fury and wrath," see the comment above on 14:10.

16:20 Describing the parting of the Red Sea and the stopping of the Jordan, the psalmist says, "The mountains skipped like rams; the hills, like the lambs of the flock" (114:4). In the face of God's judgement on Rome, the islands and mountains react, dramatizing the proportions of this act of divine judgement.

16:21 "Large hailstones like huge weights came down . . . on people": The seventh of the Egyptian plagues was that of the killer hailstorm. Now, after passing up all chances to repent, "they blasphemed God," thus sealing their fate forever.

THINKING ALOUD

John, having described God's warnings of impending judgement (the seven trumpets) now describes their execution, again paralleling the plagues of Egypt to some extent. He ties the Exodus event to this deliverance of God's people from Rome by having the saints in heaven sing the song of Moses, and by referring to the temple in heaven in terms of Moses' tent rather than Solomon's Temple.

Perhaps a story from Rabbi Nahman of Bratslov is appropriate here. The children of Israel had crossed the Red Sea and Pharaoh's army was drowned. The angels of heaven sang for joy until God silenced them: "Are not the Egyptians my creation, my children as well?"

John's outlook is primarily apocalyptic, seeing no hope in present human history. This outlook was and is very popular in times of hardship. The prophetic outlook saw hope for history based on the righteous remnant of God's faithful people. This viewpoint is popular when things are going well. Will the pendulum always swing from one to the other, or is there a middle viewpoint?

Section 6: Babylon and Her Fall

In this section John continues his comparison of Rome with Babylon and describes the mourning of the nations because of her fall.

A. The Immoral Woman and the Beast (ch. 17)

V. The Punishment of Babylon and The Destruction of Pagan Nations

17 Babylon the Great ¹Then one of the seven angels who were holding the seven bowls came and said to me, "Come here. I will show you the judgment on the great harlot who lives near the many waters. ²The kings of the earth have had intercourse with her, and the inhabitants of the earth became drunk on the wine of her harlotry." ³Then he carried me away in spirit to a deserted place where I saw a woman seated on a scarlet beast that was covered with blasphemous names, with seven heads and ten horns. ⁴The woman was wearing purple and scarlet and adorned with gold, precious stones, and pearls. She held in her hand a gold cup that was filled with the abominable and sordid deeds of her harlotry. ⁵On her forehead was written a name, which is a mystery, "Babylon the great, the mother of harlots and of the abominations of the earth." ⁶I saw that the woman was drunk on the blood of the holy ones and on the blood of the witnesses to Jesus.

Meaning of the Beast and Harlot When I saw her I was greatly amazed. ⁷The angel said to me, "Why are you amazed? I will explain to you the mystery of the woman and of the beast that carries her, the beast with the seven heads and the ten horns. ⁸The beast that you saw existed once but now exists no longer. It will come up from the abyss and is headed for destruction. The inhabitants of the earth whose names have not been written in the book of life from the foundation of the world shall be amazed when they see the beast, because it existed once but exists no longer, and yet it will come again. ⁹Here is a clue for one who has wisdom. The seven heads represent seven hills upon which the woman sits. They also represent seven kings: ¹⁰five have already fallen, one still lives, and the last has not yet come, and when he comes he must remain only a short while. ¹¹The beast that existed once but exists no longer is an eighth king, but really belongs to the seven and is headed for destruction. ¹²The ten horns that you saw represent ten kings who have not yet been crowned; they will receive royal authority along with the beast for one hour. ¹³They are of one mind and will give their power and authority to the beast. ¹⁴They will fight with the Lamb, but the Lamb will conquer them, for he is Lord of lords and king of kings, and those with him are called, chosen, and faithful.''

¹⁵Then he said to me, ''The waters that you saw where the harlot lives represent large numbers of peoples, nations, and tongues. ¹⁶The ten horns that you saw and the beast will hate the harlot; they will leave her desolate and naked; they will eat her flesh and consume her with fire. ¹⁷For God has put it into their minds to carry out his purpose and to make them come to an agreement to give their kingdom to the beast until the words of God are accomplished. ¹⁸The woman whom you saw represents the great city that has sovereignty over the kings of the earth.''

17:1 **''the great harlot''**: Consistent with his use of the Old Testament metaphor of idolatry as adultery, this is what John calls Rome, a city worshipped throughout the eastern Empire as Roma, the *magna mater* (great mother). Nahum called Nineveh a whore because of its immorality (Nah 3:4), and Isaiah called Tyre the same because of its worldliness (Isa 23:15). The woman here stands in sharp contrast to the woman we saw in chapter 12.

She **''lives near many waters.''** Jeremiah described Babylon in this way (Jer 51:13), referring to the Tigris and the Euphrates, as well as to Babylon's extensive irrigation canals. Rome may justly be called this as well, considering her maritime might, both military and commercial.

17:2 "The kings of the earth have had intercourse with her": Continuing the metaphor of idolatry as an illicit sexual relationship, John refers to the fact that all the nations of the known world had compromised with Rome and with Rome's gods in order to maintain some semblance of home rule. The obligatory statue of Zeus or some other old-order god was placed in the temples of every nation Rome conquered (except Judea, where they had to make an exception in order to keep the peace).

"the inhabitants of the earth became drunk on the wine of her harlotry": Jeremiah speaks of Babylon in this way (Jer 51:7). What a vivid image—all the kings and merchants of the world intoxicated by the might and wealth of Rome, intoxicated to the point that all moral judgement is impaired.

17:3 John goes to "a deserted place," which we saw in chapter 12 represents a place of safety. It is only from this safe vantage point that John can observe Babylon/Rome.

"a scarlet beast": This beast shows its true colors—it is the same color as the dragon representing Satan.

"covered with blasphemous names, with seven heads and ten horns": This is the beast we saw rising up out of the sea in chapter 13, where it represented the Roman emperor (see comment there for more detail).

17:4 "purple and scarlet": Purple is the color of royalty, and scarlet throughout the Bible is the color of wealth and, just as frequently, of immorality. Her robes, however, fail in contrast to those of Mother Israel/Church, who is clothed with the radiance of the sun. They also stand in stark contrast to the simple white robes which are given to the redeemed in heaven.

"adorned with gold, precious stones, and pearls": The *Testament of Judah*, written around B.C. 200–100, says that Bathshua's father, in order to attract Judah to her, "decked her in gold and pearls, and made her pour out wine for us in a feast. The wine perverted my eyesight; pleasure darkened my heart" (13:5-6). This certainly describes the whore who is Rome, who seduced the nations with her riches.

"gold cup . . . filled with the abominable and sordid deeds of her harlotry": The Greek word for "abominable" is the same word used to describe the "abomination of abominations" mentioned earlier in 11:2-3. The Greek word for "sordid" refers to the realm of the demonic, which, for John and the early Christians, was the world of false gods and idols. Therefore, it also refers to idolatry.

17:5 "On her forehead was written a name": Roman prostitutes wore a label on their foreheads with their name on it. In contrast to those who have the name of God and the new name of the Lamb written on their foreheads, this whore bears the name of one of the most wicked cities that ever existed, Babylon, which symbolizes another wicked city, Rome.

"which is a mystery": "Mystery," like "spiritually" in 11:8 above, means "a symbol."

17:6 "the woman was drunk on the blood of the holy ones": This expression, to be drunk on blood, was common in the literature of the ancient world. Isaiah 34:6, speaking of God's judgement against the nations, says, "The LORD has a sword filled with blood . . ."

This verse refers to the many Christians killed under Nero's and Domitian's persecutions, besides all the others.

"I was greatly amazed": Like the peoples of the earth, John finds Rome, no matter how wicked, still amazing to behold. Christians, in their opposition to evil, must retain a healthy respect for the attraction and ability to amaze that the power of evil retains.

17:7 John really shouldn't be amazed at the beast; the angel is now going to explain the beast's identity to him and, through him, to the reader, just in case the reader hasn't gotten the picture yet. (This repetition is didactic—Rome is being described here yet again, just as it was described above in chapter 13.)

17:8 "existed once but now exists no longer": The beast stands in sharp contrast to Christ who was and is and is to come.

"It will come up from the abyss, and is headed for destruction": Once again John describes the Nero Redivivus myth, the expectation that Nero would return, and in so doing he once again describes the past as if it were yet to happen. When the new Nero appears, he is destined for destruction.

17:9   "Here is a clue for one who has wisdom": This is very similar to the sentence that preceded the number of the beast in 13:18, and suggests that we are talking about the same person.

"seven heads . . . seven hills": Rome was and is commonly known as the city set upon seven hills.

"seven kings": We have already identified these as the seven Roman emperors from B.C. 27 (the end of the Republic) up to but not including Domitian (see comment above on 13:1). The Roman emperors following B.C. 27 were:

1. Augustus (B.C. 13–14 A.D.)
2. Tiberius (14–37)
3. Caligula (37–41)
4. Claudius (41–54)
5. Nero (54–68)
   [Galba (68–69), Otho, and Vitellius (69)]
6. Vespasian (69–79)
7. Titus (79–81)
8. Domitian (81–96)

17:10   "five have already fallen": John continues to speak in the past tense. The five are the first five up through Nero. Then comes Vespasian (skipping the three military pretenders to the throne). "The last has not yet come . . . he must remain only a short while." Titus, who destroyed the Temple in Jerusalem, ruled only for three years.

17:11   "existed once but exists no longer is an eighth king, but really belongs to the seven": Nero used to be and no longer is; in John's description Nero returned in the person of Domitian, the eighth emperor since the Republic. And, Domitian is "headed for destruction."

17:12-13   The **"ten horns"** come from Daniel. Previously (ch. 13) the horns were not identified or described except as each having a crown, so that they were either simply symbols for complete power, or they specifically represented all ten Roman leaders since the Republic. Here we have a further description of the horns as "ten kings who have not yet received a kingdom." In this context these horns represent provincial rulers who will rule with the "authority" of the beast, Domitian, for only "one hour," that is, a short time. A further clue that these horns represent Roman provincial rulers is that such rulers were in office for only one year at a time.

17:14 John says that the provincial rulers will make war on Christ, but that Christ will defeat them.

"called, chosen, and faithful": The followers of Christ have responded to God's invitation to health and salvation in Christ. Therefore God has chosen them to receive that salvation, and in turn they have been faithful to God. This is an encouragement to John's readers.

17:16 Here is one of the most striking depictions in all of Scripture of the self-destructiveness of evil. The woman is Rome and the beast the Roman Empire. John anticipates that the provincial governors will not long stand for the utter depravity of the beast and will rise up against it, shamefully exposing it to the world and burning the city of Rome. The horns of the beast have destroyed the whore, and the self-destructiveness of evil is shown forth.

17:17 The Old Testament portrays the sovereign God as completely in control, and doing such things as making the Pharaoh stubborn so that he will not repent, allowing God to punish him with more plagues. Consistent with that portrait of God, John reveals that it was God himself who made the provincial governors support the emperor in preparation for such time as "the words of God are accomplished" and they rise up to overthrow Rome. In the end willful humanity deceives itself with its own visions of power. Having made war against the Lamb, the beast turns on itself; having hurled itself against the Cross to no avail, it breaks itself thereon rather than suffer defeat, and the sovereignty of God is upheld.

17:18 Here we are finally told bluntly that the "woman" is "the great city," Rome.

B. The Fall of Babylon (18:1–19:4)

18   The Fall of Babylon ¹After this I saw another angel coming down from heaven, having great authority, and the earth became illumined by his splendor. ²He cried out in a mighty voice:

"Fallen, fallen is Babylon the great.
　She has become a haunt for demons.
　She is a cage for every unclean spirit,
　　a cage for every unclean bird,
　　[a cage for every unclean] and disgusting
　　　[beast].
³ For all the nations have drunk
　　the wine of her licentious passion.
　The kings of the earth had intercourse with
　　　her,
　　and the merchants of the earth grew rich
　　　from her drive for luxury."

⁴Then I heard another voice from heaven say:

"Depart from her, my people,
　so as not to take part in her sins
　and receive a share in her plagues,
⁵ for her sins are piled up to the sky,
　and God remembers her crimes.
⁶ Pay her back as she has paid others.
　Pay her back double for her deeds.
　Into her cup pour double what she poured.
⁷ To the measure of her boasting and wantonness
　repay her in torment and grief;
　for she said to herself,
　'I sit enthroned as queen;
　I am no widow,
　and I will never know grief.'
⁸ Therefore, her plagues will come in one day,
　pestilence, grief, and famine;
　she will be consumed by fire.
　For mighty is the Lord God who judges
　　her."

⁹The kings of the earth who had intercourse with her in their wantonness will weep and mourn over her when they see the smoke of her pyre. ¹⁰They will keep their distance for fear of the torment inflicted on her, and they will say:

"Alas, alas, great city,
    Babylon, mighty city.
    In one hour your judgment has come."

[11]The merchants of the earth will weep and mourn for her, because there will be no more markets for their cargo: [12]their cargo of gold, silver, precious stones, and pearls; fine linen, purple silk, and scarlet cloth; fragrant wood of every kind, all articles of ivory and all articles of the most expensive wood, bronze, iron, and marble; [13]cinnamon, spice, incense, myrrh, and frankincense; wine, olive oil, fine flour, and wheat; cattle and sheep, horses and chariots, and slaves, that is, human beings.

[14]"The fruit you craved
    has left you.
All your luxury and splendor are gone,
    never again will one find them."

[15]The merchants who deal in these goods, who grew rich from her, will keep their distance for fear of the torment inflicted on her. Weeping and mourning, [16]they cry out:

"Alas, alas, great city,
    wearing fine linen, purple and scarlet,
    adorned [in] gold, precious stones, and
        pearls.
[17] In one hour this great wealth has been ruined."

Every captain of a ship, every traveler at sea, sailors, and seafaring merchants stood at a distance [18]and cried out when they saw the smoke of her pyre, "What city could compare with the great city?" [19]They threw dust on their heads and cried out, weeping and mourning:

"Alas, alas, great city,
    in which all who had ships at sea
    grew rich from her wealth.
In one hour she has been ruined.
[20] Rejoice over her, heaven,
    you holy ones, apostles, and prophets.
For God has judged your case against her."

[21]A mighty angel picked up a stone like a huge millstone and threw it into the sea and said:

"With such force will Babylon the great city
    be thrown down,
    and will never be found again.

²² No melodies of harpists and musicians,
   flutists and trumpeters,
  will ever be heard in you again.
No craftsmen in any trade
  will ever be found in you again.
No sound of the millstone
  will ever be heard in you again.
²³ No light from a lamp
  will ever be seen in you again.
No voices of bride and groom
  will ever be heard in you again.
Because your merchants were the great ones
     of the world,
   all nations were led astray by your magic
     potion.
²⁴ In her was found the blood of prophets and holy ones
   and all who have been slain on the earth.''

19 ¹After this I heard what sounded like the loud voice of a great multitude in heaven, saying:

''Alleluia!
Salvation, glory, and might belong to our
   God,
² for true and just are his judgments.
He has condemned the great harlot
  who corrupted the earth with her harlotry.
He has avenged on her the blood of his
  servants.''

³They said a second time:

''Alleluia! Smoke will rise from her forever
  and ever.''

⁴The twenty-four elders and the four living creatures fell down and worshiped God who sat on the throne, saying, ''Amen. Alleluia.''

Chapter 18:1-20 describes how Babylon (Rome) is declared to be fallen, and then describes the songs of mourning of kings, merchants, and ships' captains over her. Finally, an angel describes once again how Babylon (Rome) will fall.

This section is fairly self-explanatory. The coded symbolism of earlier chapters is not necessary here, except to continue to refer to Rome as ''Babylon.''

1. An Angel Declares Babylon To Be Fallen, And God's People Are Ordered To Leave Her (18:1-8)

18:2 "Fallen, fallen is Babylon": While at the time of John's writing Rome had not actually fallen, he saw it as a virtual *fait accompli* ready to be announced. John repeats the antiphon gleaned from the Book of Isaiah (21:9) which he used in 14:8.

"She has become a haunt for demons . . . [(and) every unclean] and disgusting [beast]": In describing Babylon's downfall Isaiah says that it will become a place where wild animals will lie down and its houses will be full of "wildcats." Satyrs (demons that resemble goats) will dance there (Isa 13:21).

18:3 On this verse, see the comment on 17:2 above.

18:4 "Depart from her, my people": With similar words Jeremiah (51:45) warned the Jews to evacuate Babylon before it was invaded.

"so as not to take part in her sins": Like Lot who was told to leave the sinful, doomed city of Sodom with no regrets, they are to leave without dabbling in her immorality.

18:6 "Into her cup pour double what she poured": See comment on 16:6.

18:7 "I will never know grief": The self-deception of evil is revealed.

18:8 "she will be consumed by fire": John foresees a swift judgement by fire, like that which befell Sodom and Gomorrah.

2. The Kings' Funeral Song over Babylon (18:9-10)

18:10 "In one hour": The hour in which the ten horns are allowed to persecute Christ is balanced with the one hour in which Rome will perish.

3. The Merchants' Funeral Song
over Babylon (18:11-17)

The song of the merchants is twice as long as that of the kings—they have much to lose with the collapse of Rome. This section mirrors Ezekiel 27.

18:12-13   Here is a catalogue of the riches of Rome, imported and exported all over the known world and beyond. It is for the loss of these that the merchants mourn, and not so much for the city itself.

18:14   John underscores the finality of the defeat of Rome.

18:17   The ''single hour'' is again mentioned.

4. The Ships' Captains' Funeral Song
over Babylon (18:18-20)

18:19   **''threw dust on their heads''**: This is an ancient sign of grief and shock.

18:20   **''God has judged your case against her''**: The sense of the Greek text is, ''God has given her the punishment she gave them.'' This echoes Jeremiah 50:15b: ''Take revenge on her, as she has done, do to her.''

In the songs of 18:9-20 John leaves his strangely symbolic world, except for the image of the whore of Babylon as Rome, and indulges in a flight of imagination. Drawing upon the defamations of Jeremiah, he portrays almost with relish the international mourning that will take place at the collapse of the Church's bitter enemy, Rome. Now, in 18:21-24 he will write Rome's obituary.

5. Babylon (Rome) is Dead (18:21-24)

18:21   **''a huge millstone''**: Drawing on an image from Jeremiah 51:63 John presents a graphic picture of the city's fall.

18:22-23   In these melancholy lines John portrays some of the pathos of Rome's destruction. Despite its wickedness,

Rome was a place of high culture as well as home to the everyday life of ordinary people.

18:23 "your magic potion": Magic and witchcraft in biblical days were believed to be demonically empowered.

18:24 Rome was responsible for the deaths of those who spoke God's word, God's own people, and all sorts of other people.

6. Heaven's Praise (19:1-4)

This scene of heavenly praise, short as it is compared to the chapter-long dirges over the city, serves as a succinct counterpart to the mourning of kings, merchants, and sea captains. Once again, in verse 2, we encounter the theme of God's avenging his people. While this sounds more like the Old Testament view of God, both the writings of St. Paul and the Letter to the Hebrews remind Christians not to take vengeance for themselves, because " 'Vengeance is mine, I will repay,' says the Lord" (Rom 12:19, quoting Deut 32:35, 41).

THINKING ALOUD

Chapter 17 is striking for its depiction of Rome as the whore Babylon. Rome and its culture stand in stark contrast to the way of life of the followers of the carpenter of Nazareth.

The description of the heads and horns gets complicated, but the interpretation which says that John is speaking of Domitian and the provincial kings of the east whom Domitian is trying to subjugate through his imperial cult is both simple and workable.

What should raise the eyebrows of American Christians is the similarity between ancient Rome's opulence and our own. Wealth in itself is not sinful; but the accumulation of wealth can so easily become an end in itself, indeed an end above all others, and lead to a sense of self-sufficiency which excludes God. A contemporary television cartoon character offered grace before dinner by saying, "We paid for this stuff, so thanks for nothing." This is the poison of wealth.

Section 7: The Last Things

In this final section of the book John describes the events surrounding the end of history as he foresees it.

A. The Wedding Feast of the Lamb (19:5-10)

The Victory Song   ⁵A voice coming from the throne said:
"Praise our God, all you his servants,
    [and] you who revere him, small and
        great."

⁶Then I heard something like the sound of a great multitude or the sound of rushing water or mighty peals of thunder, as they said:

    "Alleluia!
    The Lord has established his reign,
        [our] God, the almighty.
⁷ Let us rejoice and be glad
    and give him glory.
    For the wedding day of the Lamb has come,
        his bride has made herself ready.
⁸ She was allowed to wear
    a bright, clean linen garment."

(The linen represents the righteous deeds of the holy ones.)
    ⁹Then the angel said to me, "Write this: Blessed are those who have been called to the wedding feast of the Lamb." And he said to me, "These words are true; they come from God." ¹⁰I fell at his feet to worship him. But he said to me, "Don't! I am a fellow servant of yours and of your brothers who bear witness to Jesus. Worship God. Witness to Jesus is the spirit of prophecy."

19:5   With this adaptation of Psalm 134:1 John begins the final section of the book by praising God.

"you who revere him": "Revere," translated in other versions as "fear," refers to the fear that grows out of a deep respect, not the dread that fears harm or grows out of mistrust. It is this healthy respect, according to Job 28:28, Psalm 111:10, and Proverbs 1:7, which is the seed of wisdom and the beginning of understanding.

19:6 **"a great multitude"**: These are the redeemed, as in 7:9. The "sound of rushing water or mighty peals of thunder" are signs of the divine power that surrounded and redeemed this crowd. Recall that in 1:15 the voice of Christ was described as sounding like rushing water.

John takes part two of this verse, which is the beginning of the next song, from Psalm 97:1. The King James Version of it reads, "Alleluia: for the Lord God omnipotent reigneth" (which provides part of the text for Handel's "Hallelujah Chorus"). "Alleluia" is taken directly from the Hebrew word "hallelu-jah," which means "praise to Yah" (which is short for Yahweh, God's sacred name).

The word for "almighty" in Greek is *pantocrator*, a favorite word of John in Revelation, and often used in the early Church for Christ. It literally means "sovereign, powerful in every way."

19:7 **"The wedding day of the Lamb"**: Israel's relationship with God is often pictured in the Old Testament (especially in Hosea) as being like that of a wife and husband. In the apocryphal book 4 Ezra, the new Jerusalem is portrayed as a woman.

Jesus often described the kingdom of God in parables about weddings, including one in which a king gives a wedding banquet for his son (Matt 22:1ff.). Jesus and John the Baptizer both refer to Jesus as a bridegroom. The Church is compared to a bride by St. Paul in 2 Corinthians 11:2: "I betrothed you to one husband to present you as a chaste virgin to Christ."

19:8 **"linen"**: John uses, and then explains, the image of a fine linen dress. This mirrors the white robe given to individual Christians described in earlier chapters.

19:9 Again John is told to **"Write this."** Here the bride and the guests at the **"wedding feast"** are the same persons, illustrating the fluidity of John's imagery. 4 Ezra speaks of the wedding feast as taking place when the full roll of the saints is completed, an idea we saw in 6:11.

"feast": The coming of God's kingdom in its fullness is described by the prophet Isaiah as a banquet, sometimes called the messianic banquet: "On this mountain the Lord of hosts will provide for all peoples a feast of rich food and choice wines, juicy, rich food and pure, choice wine" (Isa 25:6). John continues this idea as he foresees the joys that await the faithful. (The Holy Eucharist is often described as a foretaste of this heavenly banquet.)

19:10   Some have seen in this verse a strict warning against worshipping angels, something St. Paul warned the Colossian church against (Col 2:8).

"Worship God": The command to worship only God has been a clear, consistent, significant part of John's message to his readers, and he wants them to know that this excludes not only idols and Roman emperors, but the holy angels as well.

"Witness to Jesus is the spirit of prophecy": 1 John 4:1 speaks of testing the spirits to see whether they are from God, and here John is saying that a witness (or, testimony) to Jesus is at the heart of any true spirit of prophecy. The words *testimony* and *witness* are both contained in the Greek word *martyria* from which we get our word *martyr*. The "testimony of Jesus" is the proclamation in word and example by John and the churches that Jesus is the Son of God and the Savior of the world, God incarnate, the light of life, the true and living way.

B. The Rider on the White Horse Defeats the Beast and his Armies (19:11-21)

The King of Kings   ¹¹Then I saw the heavens opened, and there was a white horse; its rider was [called] "Faithful and True." He judges and wages war in righteousness. ¹²His eyes were [like] a fiery flame, and on his head were many diadems. He had a name inscribed that no one knows except himself. ¹³He wore a cloak that had been dipped in blood, and his name was called the Word of God. ¹⁴The armies of heaven followed him, mounted on white horses and wearing clean white linen. ¹⁵Out of his mouth came a sharp sword to strike the nations. He will rule them with an iron rod, and he himself will tread out in the wine press the wine of the fury and wrath of God the almighty. ¹⁶He has a name written on his cloak and on his thigh, "King of kings and Lord of lords."

¹⁷Then I saw an angel standing on the sun. He cried out [in] a loud voice to all the birds flying high overhead, "Come here. Gather for God's great feast, ¹⁸to eat the flesh of kings, the flesh of military officers, and the flesh of warriors, the flesh of horses and of their riders, and the flesh of all, free and slave, small and great." ¹⁹Then I saw the beast and the kings of the earth and their armies gathered to fight against the one riding the horse and against his army. ²⁰The beast was caught and with it the false prophet who had performed in its sight the signs by which he led astray those who had accepted the mark of the beast and those who had worshiped its image. The two were thrown alive into the fiery pool burning with sulfur. ²¹The rest were killed by the sword that came out of the mouth of the one riding the horse, and all the birds gorged themselves on their flesh.

Here we have a very clear example of how John does not follow a strict time line. Whereas elsewhere in Revelation he described past and present events as if they were both yet to occur (ch. 12), here he describes the defeat of the beast's hosts (which was described as a grape harvest beginning at 14:14) as if it had not yet happened. The link is 19:15, "he himself will tread out the wine press the wine of the fury and wrath of God the almighty," a close parallel to 14:19.

19:11 A "white horse" was (and still is) traditionally ridden by a monarch, a general, or some other hero.

"Faithful and True": Jesus is called "the faithful witness" in 1:5, "the holy one, the true" in 3:7, and "the faithful and true witness" in 3:14. These are two of Jesus' most important titles for John; as John has repeatedly called upon the Christians to remain faithful and true to Christ, so he emphasizes that Christ will be faithful and true to them.

19:12 **"His eyes were [like] a fiery flame"**: We saw this description of Christ in 1:14.

"on his head were many diadems": In contrast to the beast which only has ten crowns, Christ has many.

"a name . . . no one knows but himself": In 3:12 Christ promised the Philadelphians "my own name," with no mention about whether they would know what it is. Perhaps the simplest interpretation of the unknown name lies in the idea which was widespread among many ancient nations (including Israel) that to know the name of a god or demon was to have power over him. Therefore, no one shall know Christ's new name, for no one will have mastery over him.

19:13 "a cloak that had been dipped in blood": Note Isaiah 63:1-4, in which God's garments are red like those of the wine presser because he has just trampled his enemies.

How can the blood on his garment be the blood of his enemies if he hasn't killed them yet (verse 15 below says that he *will* tread out the winepress)? The simplest explanation is that, just as Christ in 1:7 bears the marks of his crucifixion, so his garments are here stained with the blood of the martyrs whom he has embraced and welcomed into the heavenly kingdom. He comes spattered with the blood of his beloved ones to press the grapes of God's wrath against those who inflicted such a slaughter. See comment on 14:20.

"the Word of God": Of all the titles and names given to Jesus, this one is special to the books in the New Testament that bear the name of John, especially the Gospel of John, where Jesus is the Word made flesh.

19:15 "a sharp sword": Seen in 1:16, this sword represents his word of judgement against sinners.

"rule with an iron rod": Seen above in 2:27 and found originally in Isaiah, this refers to the authority which God will give the Messiah over the nations.

"tread out in the winepress": See above, 14:19.

19:16 "King of kings and Lord of lords": Mentioned before in 17:14, this title proclaims the absolute dominion and power of Christ over all rulers and nations of the earth.

19:19 "the kings of the earth": These are the kings represented by the ten horns in chapter 13.

19:20 John reminds us of the identity of the false prophet, described above in 13:14ff. as the second beast. The false prophet is the emperor worship cult and its leaders.

"thrown alive into the fiery pool burning with sulphur": In the apocalyptic book 1 Enoch the angels that sinned as well as all false prophets, blasphemers, and evildoers will be punished forever in a desert pit filled with fire.

19:21 "killed by the sword that came out of the mouth of the one riding the horse": The followers of the Roman emperor and his cult were dispatched simply by the word of judgement which Christ spoke. Recalling that God called the worlds into existence merely by uttering a word of command, by a simple word of judgement Christ is portrayed balancing the scales of divine justice.

The beast and the false prophet experience the immediate execution of their sentence; their followers are sentenced, with the sentence being carried out in the second death (in 20:14).

"all the birds gorged themselves": The picture is that of the aftermath of a battle, when vultures and other birds of prey flocked to the battlefield to feed upon the bodies of the fallen.

John may have had in mind the apocalyptic 1 Enoch 41:1-6, which describes the judgement upon the kings of the earth by the Son of Man.

THINKING ALOUD

John announces the wedding feast of the Lamb, and recaps once again the defeat of Rome. This leads us to two different meditations.

Though much sentiment surrounds weddings, we may nevertheless profit from thinking about the Church as the spouse of Christ. Christ is the faithful and true spouse; how faithful and true has the Church been throughout the centuries? Even as a human marriage relationship must be maintained with hard work, so must the Church's relationship with Christ.

The Roman Empire, as we know, did not fall as John expected. However, two things did happen: Domitian's persecutions were over within a year or so of the writing of Revelation, and, for better or for worse, Christianity became the official religion of Rome under Constantine in the fourth century. Thus, in a sense, Christ did conquer Rome, but not quite in the way John describes.

Sometimes we sense how things will turn out, but do we sometimes go too far in insisting that they work themselves out in just one certain way?

C. The Millennium and the Defeat of Satan (20:1-10)

20   The Thousand-year Reign   ¹Then I saw an angel come down from heaven, holding in his hand the key to the abyss and a heavy chain. ²He seized the dragon, the ancient serpent, which is the Devil or Satan, and tied it up for a thousand years ³and threw it into the abyss, which he locked over it and sealed, so that it could no longer lead the nations astray until the thousand years are completed. After this, it is to be released for a short time.

⁴Then I saw thrones; those who sat on them were entrusted with judgment. I also saw the souls of those who had been beheaded for their witness to Jesus and for the word of God, and who had not worshiped the beast or its image nor had accepted its mark on their foreheads or hands. They came to life and they reigned with Christ for a thousand years. ⁵The rest of the dead did not come to life until the thousand years were over. This is the first resurrection. ⁶Blessed and holy is the one who shares in the first resurrection. The second death has no power over these; they will be priests of God and of Christ, and they will reign with him for [the] thousand years.

⁷When the thousand years are completed, Satan will be released from his prison. ⁸He will go out to deceive the nations at the four corners of the earth, Gog and Magog, to gather them for battle; their number is like the sand of the sea. ⁹They invaded the breadth of the earth and surrounded the camp of the holy ones and the beloved city. But fire came down from heaven and consumed them. ¹⁰The Devil who had led them astray was thrown into the pool of fire and sulfur, where the beast and the false prophet were. There they will be tormented day and night forever and ever.

Chapter 20 introduces the thousand-year imprisonment of the dragon, which coincides with the thousand-year reign of Christ and all the faithful witnesses to Christ. A great deal of discussion and many gallons of ink have been devoted to various explanations of this number, from the earliest days of the Church down to the present.

20:1 **"an angel . . . holding in his hand the key to the abyss":** This is Uriel the archangel, whom we saw in 9:1.

20:2-3 Uriel seizes "the dragon" (again identified with the "serpent" in the garden of Eden) and imprisons him for a **"thousand years."** No longer can he "lead the nations astray."

This thousand years is known in Christian theology as the millennium (from the Latin for "one thousand years"). Like the other numbers in the Book of Revelation, this number is also symbolic: 10 represents completeness, 3 represents holiness, so 10 x 10 x 10 = 1000. This is the holy reign of Christ in all its fullness.

Just as we noted that the destruction of the city was described three different times in several different ways, so the victory of Christ was described in chapters 5, 12, and 19, as well as here, and the throwing down of Satan twice, including here. John repeats for emphasis and varies his symbolism in order to illuminate various aspects of his message. This thousand years represents the victory over Satan by Christ through his obedient death and glorious resurrection. As G. K. Chesterton suggested, the weekend of that first Good Friday and Easter was D-Day, and we are living in the time of mopping-up operations, as it were. The thousand years is now, for Christ rules now in the hearts of those who obey him. The victory has been won; we await only its final realization on earth as in heaven.

"After this, it is to be released for a short time": Satan is defeated, but not destroyed. Christ has forever chained the dragon, but every time a human heart, exercising the free will which God gave us all, chooses evil over good, the dragon's chains are loosened.

20:4 Christ empowers political authority to exercise righteousness, as St. Paul describes in his epistles. The testimony of those who died for Christ is not dead; it lives throughout the ages, even as the saints themselves share life with Christ in paradise.

20:5-6 **"The rest of the dead did not come to life until the thousand years were over"**: St. Paul (in 1 Cor 15:20) called Christ "the firstfruits of those who have fallen asleep." John in Revelation 14:4 described the faithful witnesses to Christ, symbolized as the 144,000, as those who "have been ransomed as the firstfruits of the human race for God and the Lamb." Those who died for their witness to Christ are the firstfruits, sharing in the first resurrection. The second resurrection is unto judgement.

"The second death": Physical death is the first death, spiritual death the second.

20:7-9 **"Satan will be released"** in order to **"deceive the nations at the four corners of the earth, Gog and Magog."** In Ezekiel 38 and 39, Gog is the prince of the land of Magog. There "Gog and Magog" symbolize all of Israel's enemies. So also here in Revelation they represent the distant lands beyond the empire of the defeated beast (e.g., the Parthians) that do not submit to the Lamb and to the martyrs. They assail "the camp of the holy ones," symbolizing the assaults of evil upon God's people despite Christ's victory on the cross; but evil does not prevail. "Fire," sign of heavenly judgement, rains down upon them all and destroys them.

20:10 Now "the Devil" at long last joins the beast and the false prophet in "the pool of fire and sulphur." Unlike the others who are destroyed outright, this unholy trinity is "tormented day and night forever and ever."

THINKING ALOUD

To take this chapter literally and use it to try to construct blueprints of the future is to ignore and trivialize the basic truth here. This planet and the peoples on it were destined from the beginning to be like Eden, but we fell away from the path by following our own self-interests. Christ won the victory in his cross and resurrection. Are we to sit back and wait for him to bring his kingdom, or shall we "put legs on our prayers" when we say, "Thy kingdom come on earth as it is in heaven"? The deceiver is among us, but so is the victorious Lamb and the promise.

D. The Final Judgement (20:11-15)

The Large White Throne ¹¹Next I saw a large white throne and the one who was sitting on it. The earth and the sky fled from his presence and there was no place for them. ¹²I saw the dead, the great and the lowly, standing before the throne, and scrolls were opened. Then another scroll was opened, the book of life. The dead were judged according to their deeds, by what was written in the scrolls. ¹³The sea gave up its dead; then Death and Hades gave up their dead. All the dead were judged according to their deeds. ¹⁴Then Death and Hades were thrown into the pool of fire. (This pool of fire is the second death.)¹⁵ Anyone whose name was not found written in the book of life was thrown into the pool of fire.

20:11 **"large white throne"**: The first thing John reported seeing in heaven was a throne with God seated upon it (4:2). Now he sees it again. It is "white" with the radiance and splendor of the thrice-holy God.

"The earth and heaven fled": Since 21:1 tells us that "the first heaven and the first earth had disappeared," we may assume that it is here that they did the disappearing.

20:12 **"scrolls were opened"**: Daniel 7:10b says, "The court was convened, and the books were opened."

"the book of life": As in 3:5, this is the citizenship rollbook of the New Jerusalem.

20:13 **"Death and Hades"**: Hades is the Greek equivalent for the Hebrew Sheol, the pit, the realm of death where all departed spirits were believed to go.

20:14-15 **"thrown into the pool of fire"**: Whereas the unholy trinity are described as burning forever in pain, these verses imply destruction. There is no more death, there is no more pit, for death has been destroyed and all its darkened realm.

"the second death": That is, spiritual death.

THINKING ALOUD

The Book of Hebrews says, "it is appointed that human beings die once, and after this the judgment" (9:27). Many people do not fear judgement, they only fear getting caught. This is not a matter of getting caught. Everyone dies, then comes judgement. Strangely, it is not those who fear judgement who should worry. Most people who fear judgement do so because they respect God and seek to live according to his ways. It is those with utterly no sense of accountability for their actions who will receive a real surprise at the judgement.

E. *The New Heaven and the New Earth (21:1-8)*

VI. The New Creation

21 The New Heaven and the New Earth ¹Then I saw a new heaven and a new earth. The former heaven and the former earth had passed away, and the sea was no more. ²I also saw the holy city, a new Jerusalem, coming down out of heaven from God, prepared as a bride adorned for her husband. ³I heard a loud voice from the throne saying, "Behold, God's dwelling is with the human race. He will dwell with them and they will be his people and God himself will always be with them [as their God]. ⁴He will wipe every tear from their eyes, and there shall be no more death or mourning, wailing or pain, [for] the old order has passed away."

⁵The one who sat on the throne said, "Behold, I make all things new." Then he said, "Write these words down, for they are trustworthy and true." ⁶He said to me, "They are accomplished. I [am] the Alpha and the Omega, the beginning and the end. To the thirsty I will give a gift from the spring of life-giving water. ⁷The victor will inherit these gifts, and I shall be his God, and he will be my son. ⁸But as for cowards, the unfaithful, the depraved, murderers, the unchaste, sorcerers, idol-worshipers, and deceivers of every sort, their lot is in the burning pool of fire and sulfur, which is the second death."

21:1 "a new heaven and a new earth": Isaiah 65:17-18 says, "Lo, I am about to create new heavens and a new earth; The things of the past shall not be remembered or come to mind. Instead, there shall always be rejoicing and happiness in what I create; For I create Jerusalem to be a joy and its people to be a delight.'' This beautiful vision is the basis for the way John portrays the New Jerusalem.

21:2 "the holy city, a new Jerusalem, coming down out of heaven from God": The New Jerusalem is the counterpart to the heavenly temple we have been seeing throughout Revelation.

"prepared as a bride adorned for her husband": See comment on 19:7-8 above.

21:3 "God's dwelling is with the human race": Whereas God's home was with his people in the sacred tent in the desert and in the Temple in Jerusalem, now his heavenly home, the New Jerusalem, has descended to the new earth. Whereas before the transcendence of God was emphasized, his immanence is now primary.

21:4 This verse is taken from Isaiah 65 (see quotation at 21:1 above). It has been a comfort to countless Christians through the ages at times of bereavement and personal loss.

21:5 "Behold, I make all things new": In Galatians and in 2 Corinthians St. Paul says, ''So, whoever is in Christ is a new creation: the old things have passed away; behold, new things have come'' (2 Cor 5:17). Here in Revelation he renews the entire creation.

"Write these words down": John was told to write down the vision he would see (the Book of Revelation), the messages to the seven churches, the beatitude concerning those who die in the Lord and those who are invited to the supper of the Lamb. Now he is told to write for the last time.

"for they are trustworthy and true": This is a repeated theme in Revelation.

21:6 "They are accomplished": This is very similar to the words of Jesus on the cross the moment before he died, according to the Gospel of John. In Christ, everything comes to its full perfection and completion.

"the Alpha and the Omega": This is the way God first identified himself to John in 1:8 (see comment there).

"I will give a gift from the spring of life-giving water": Jesus in the Gospel of John says to the woman at the well, "the water I shall give will become in him a spring of water welling up to eternal life" (4:14).

21:7 "I shall be his God, and he will be my son": In 2 Samuel 7 God promises to David that he will have a son. He says to David of that son, "I will be a father to him, and he shall be a son to me" (7:14). Jesus holds the keys of David, and all who triumph through him become God's spiritual sons and daughters.

21:8 In another warning to any persons reading Revelation who are yet unrepentant, John catalogues the sins which will result in spiritual death. It is important to note, as in similar lists elsewhere in the New Testament, that the Scriptures are speaking of those who make these sins their life's practice.

F. The New Jerusalem (21:9–22:5)

The New Jerusalem ⁹One of the seven angels who held the seven bowls filled with the seven last plagues came and said to me, "Come here. I will show you the bride, the wife of the Lamb." ¹⁰He took me in spirit to a great, high mountain and showed me the holy city Jerusalem coming down out of heaven from God. ¹¹It gleamed with the splendor of God. Its radiance was like that of a precious stone, like jasper, clear as crystal. ¹²It had a massive, high wall, with twelve gates where twelve angels were stationed and on which names were inscribed, [the names] of the twelve tribes of the Israelites. ¹³There were three gates facing east, three north, three south, and three west. ¹⁴The wall of the city had twelve courses of stones as its foundation, on which were inscribed the twelve names of the twelve apostles of the Lamb.

¹⁵The one who spoke to me held a gold measuring rod to measure the city, its gates, and its wall. ¹⁶The city was square, its length the same as [also] its width. He measured the city with the rod and found it fifteen hundred miles in length and width and height. ¹⁷He also measured its wall: one hundred and forty-four cubits according to the standard unit of measurement the angel used. ¹⁸The wall was constructed of jasper, while the city was pure gold, clear as glass.

¹⁹The foundations of the city wall were decorated with every precious stone; the first course of stones was jasper, the second sapphire, the third chalcedony, the fourth emerald, ²⁰the fifth sardonyx, the sixth carnelian, the seventh chrysolite, the eighth beryl, the ninth topaz, the tenth chrysoprase, the eleventh hyacinth, and the twelfth amethyst. ²¹The twelve gates were twelve pearls, each of the gates made from a single pearl; and the street of the city was of pure gold, transparent as glass.

²²I saw no temple in the city, for its temple is the Lord God almighty and the Lamb. ²³The city had no need of sun or moon to shine on it, for the glory of God gave it light, and its lamp was the Lamb. ²⁴The nations will walk by its light, and to it the kings of the earth will bring their treasure. ²⁵During the day its gates will never be shut, and there will be no night there. ²⁶The treasure and wealth of the nations will be brought there, ²⁷but nothing unclean will enter it, nor any[one] who does abominable things or tells lies. Only those will enter whose names are written in the Lamb's book of life.

22 ¹Then the angel showed me the river of life-giving water, sparkling like crystal, flowing from the throne of God and of the Lamb ²down the middle of its street. On either side of the river grew the tree of life that produces fruit twelve times a year, once each month; the leaves of the trees serve as medicine for the nations. ³Nothing accursed will be found there anymore. The throne of God and of the Lamb will be in it, and his servants will worship him. ⁴They will look upon his face, and his name will be on their foreheads. ⁵Night will be no more, nor will they need light from lamp or sun, for the Lord God shall give them light, and they shall reign forever and ever.

21:10 "a great, high mountain": John is preparing to describe for us his vision of the New Jerusalem, which parallels in many ways the description of the New Temple in Ezekiel 40. There Ezekiel says, "the hand of the Lord . . . brought me in divine visions to the land of Israel, where he set me down on a very high mountain. On it there seemed to be a city being built before me" (40:1b-2). What Ezekiel saw was the New Jerusalem and its Temple. John links his vision with Ezekiel's using the "mountain." (In both passages we are reminded of how God brought Moses up onto the mountain to look over into the Promised Land.)

21:11 **"like jasper"**: God was described in 4:3 as like a jasper. A jasper is often greenish in color, the color of life.

21:12-13 **"twelve gates"**: Ezekiel's holy city also had twelve gates for each of the twelve tribes of Israel (48:30). John describes this city like Ezekiel's, with three gates on each of the four sides. The significance is that God's people have universal access to his city.

21:14 Ephesians 2:20 says that the household of God is "built upon the foundation of the apostles and prophets."

21:16 **"square"**: According to 1 Kings 6:20, in Solomon's Temple the holy of holies (the inner room where the ark of the covenant was kept and where God was believed to live) was a cube. In times past only the high priest could enter the holy of holies where the Creator of heaven and earth lived, and only once a year at that. In the world to come the holy of holies is expanded so that all of God's people live in it with him.

"fifteen hundred miles": To understand this dimension we must go back to the Greek text, which says "twelve thousand stadia" (stadia were the Roman equivalent of miles; one of them was a "stadium"). Here again is the number twelve thousand, which is twelve (the number of patriarchs and of apostles, signifying God's people) times one thousand, the ancient equivalent of saying "a jillion." This holy place is large enough for all of God's people.

21:17 **"its wall: one hundred and forty-four cubits"**: Here is the number 144 again, twelve times twelve, representing all of God's people. (A cubit was around eighteen inches, equivalent to a foot.) Every ancient city had a wall, and this one is walled about symbolically with patriarchs and apostles!

It is to be noted here that the ancient Greek writer Herodotus describes the ancient city of Babylon in words very similar to those of John's description of the New Jerusalem. It is reasonable to conclude that John knew of Herodotus's description and cleverly used it to point out that the New Jerusalem is what Babylon could only try to be.

21:18 No earthly city could boast these materials, which are designed not to hide but to radiate the glory of the Holy One who dwells within.

21:19-20 Exodus 28:17-20 describes the high priest's breast-plate and the twelve stones on it, representing the twelve tribes. The foundations of the New Jerusalem, which we already noted are twelve in number with the names of the twelve apostles (21:14), also include the twelve tribes of Israel. One of the earliest Christian heresies tried to eliminate the Old Testament from the Christian religion. It cannot be done—Israel is foundational to the Church.

John's list of jewels does not follow the list in Exodus, however. Rather, it follows the traditional order of the twelve stones representing the twelve signs of the zodiac in ancient Egypt and Arabia, only backwards (perhaps because John has no wish to endorse astrology).

21:21 **"The twelve gates were twelve pearls":** Isaiah 54:12 speaks of God's new relationship with Israel and says in part, "I will make . . . your gates of carbuncles" (a carbuncle is a red jewel, like a ruby). This is the origin in popular parlance of the expression "the pearly gates."

"the street of the city was of pure gold, transparent as glass": Here is the origin of the popular expression "streets of gold." John is not seeking to appeal to a hedonistic mind-set bent on enriching itself with material things. Instead, he is primarily using the gems and gold to link the New Jerusalem with the earthly Temple and Ezekiel's and Isaiah's vision of a new one. Also, for people often so lacking in the rich things of this world as many of the first Christians were, this portrays heaven, not as fulfilling their wildest dreams for riches, but as a place far surpassing anything human riches could construct.

21:22 **"I saw no temple in the city":** There was no need for a temple there: the entire city is a temple, with "the Lord God almighty and the Lamb" readily accessible to all who live there.

21:23 This verse is very similar to Isaiah 60:19.

21:24 Isaiah 60 contains the lines "Nations shall walk by your light, and kings by your shining radiance" (v. 3) and "the wealth of nations shall be brought to you" (v. 5). We are not to take this literally and try to imagine what other nations there are on earth besides the New Jerusalem; the city is being described as if it were an exalted earthly Jerusalem, in the same way that the Old Testament prophets described it. In the Old Testament, the word for "nations" was the same word used for "Gentiles." Thus, perhaps we have expressed here the promise that those once considered outside the realm of God are included as well.

21:27 Here is yet another warning to anyone reading the book who is still wavering or compromising with sin.

22:1 **"the river of life-giving water"**: Both Ezekiel (47:1ff.) and Zechariah (14:8) speak of a river of life-giving waters flowing from the temple, from the heavenly city. Psalm 46:5-6 says, "There is a stream whose runlets gladden the city of God, the holy dwelling of the Most High. God is in its midst; it shall not be disturbed." In an arid land this verse would have special meaning.

22:2 Ezekiel 47:12 contains almost an identical description. This tree is equivalent to the tree of life in the garden of Eden (Gen 3:22). Whereas there humans were barred from eating of the tree, here it is available to them year-round, and even its leaves bring healing.

22:4 **"They will look upon his face"**: This is different from life in the world where the presence of God must be mediated. "his name will be on their foreheads": See comment at 3:12.

THINKING ALOUD

The basic idea clothed in this fantastic imagery is that in the new heavens and earth we will be returned to the blessedness of Eden, with God and Christ in residence with us.

A portion of a prayer by William Penn comes to mind, words to this effect: "Lord, you have gone to prepare a place for us; prepare us for that happy place." Our task is not to try to draw diagrams of the heavenly Jerusalem or make time-lines determining its date and place of arrival. Our task is to make ourselves available to Christ in service to others so that he may prepare us for that happy place.

Epilogue and Closing (22:6-21)

VII. Epilogue

⁶And he said to me, "These words are trustworthy and true, and the Lord, the God of prophetic spirits, sent his angel to show his servants what must happen soon." ⁷"Behold, I am coming soon." Blessed is the one who keeps the prophetic message of this book.

⁸It is I, John, who heard and saw these things, and when I heard and saw them I fell down to worship at the feet of the angel who showed them to me. ⁹But he said to me, "Don't! I am a fellow servant of yours and of your brothers the prophets and of those who keep the message of this book. Worship God."

¹⁰Then he said to me, "Do not seal up the prophetic words of this book, for the appointed time is near. ¹¹Let the wicked still act wickedly, and the filthy still be filthy. The righteous must still do right, and the holy still be holy."

¹²"Behold, I am coming soon. I bring with me the recompense I will give to each according to his deeds. ¹³I am the Alpha and the Omega, the first and the last, the beginning and the end."

¹⁴Blessed are they who wash their robes so as to have the right to the tree of life and enter the city through its gates. ¹⁵Outside are the dogs, the sorcerers, the unchaste, the murderers, the idol-worshipers, and all who love and practice deceit.

¹⁶"I, Jesus, sent my angel to give you this testimony for the churches. I am the root and offspring of David, the bright morning star."

¹⁷The Spirit and the bride say, "Come." Let the hearer say, "Come." Let the one who thirsts come forward, and the one who wants it receive the gift of life-giving water.

¹⁸I warn everyone who hears the prophetic words in this book: if anyone adds to them, God will add to him the plagues described in this book, ¹⁹and if anyone takes away from the words in this prophetic book, God will take away

his share in the tree of life and in the holy city described in this book.

²⁰The one who gives this testimony says, "Yes, I am coming soon." Amen! Come, Lord Jesus!

²¹The grace of the Lord Jesus be with all.

John closes Revelation with a final word of encouragement, a warning, and a benediction.

22:6 At the end of the book John reminds the reader where the revelation in the book originated.

"what must happen soon": This is another indication that John expected all the things in his revelation to transpire very soon after he sent the book to the churches.

22:7 **"I am coming soon"**: Christ had said these words to the church at Sardis. Now he declares it openly to everyone.

"the prophetic message of this book": A prophecy is not primarily a prediction of the future; it is a disclosing of the mind of God as it pertains to current events and what God intends to do about them.

22:8 The author again identifies himself as John. See discussion on this at the beginning of the commentary.

22:9 **"Don't!"**: In 19:10 John attempted to bow down and worship the angel and was told not to do so. The repetition of that command here emphasizes the message it was meant to convey there as well: even though angels play a large part in salvation history and in doing the work of God, they are not to be worshipped.

22:10 Daniel was told to keep the contents of his book a secret because the events it describes were to happen a long time later. John is told the opposite: "the appointed time is near."

22:11 Both Ezekiel (3:27) and Daniel (12:10) contain very similar verses. It is as if they are saying, "Don't worry about other people—they're going to do what they're going to do. You focus on what you are going to do."

22:12 The imminent return of Christ is underscored, together with the promise of his reward.

22:13 See comment on 1:8.

22:14 **"wash their robes"**: 7:14 referred to the martyrs who had been faithful to the death like Christ as those who "have washed their robes and made them white in the blood of the Lamb." See additional comment there.

"fruit of the tree that gives life": This refers to the tree of life in the garden of Eden (Gen 2:9) which was described in 22:2 above.

22:15 This is another implicit warning to the sinful.

22:16 Jesus describes himself again as he did in 5:5 and 2:27 (see comments there).

22:17 **"the bride"**: The Holy Spirit's call to repentance and to faithfulness comes through the bride of Christ, the Church.

"Let the hearer say, 'Come.'": All Christians who hear the reading of this revelation and the warning of the Spirit speaking through it are to go out and warn others.

"Let the one who thirsts come forward": This refers to Isaiah 55:1 and repeats what was said to the Laodiceans in 3:18. At the end of the book John issues an invitation for people to come to the water of life, perhaps referring to baptism.

22:18 Books in John's day were rolls of parchment pages that were sewn together, the last pages of the book being on the outside of the roll. It would be very simple for someone desiring to alter the scroll either to unstitch the last panel or stitch a new one on. So John, like other authors in his day, issued a stern warning against any who would do this.

(There are some who would theologically interpret this as applying to the entire Bible, especially because it comes at the end of our Bible. However, such a reading stretches these verses out of their immediate context.)

22:20 For the third time John repeats the words of Christ, that he is coming soon. In the face of the great suffering of his people, not to mention his own imprisonment, John utters the prayer full of faith and hope which St. Paul uttered in Aramaic, the everyday language of Jesus and of Palestinian Jews, which was used at the early Christian celebrations of the Holy Eucharist: "Marana tha—Come Lord Jesus!"

22:21 **"Grace . . . be with you":** This was a very common early Christian closing. St. Paul ends almost all of his letters with some form of this.

THINKING ALOUD

For Christians beseiged by persecution, this prayer was the expression of a fond and sincere hope: "Even so, Come Lord Jesus!" The coming of Christ is a difficult subject for us. Two thousand years have lulled us into neglect of this credal truth, unless we are one of those who has the entire itinerary of the return worked out in a three-foot, five-color timeline. The fact is that Christ is present with us through the Holy Spirit in the message of Scripture, in the assembly of the faithful, and in the Holy Eucharist. When Christ returns and we ask him where he has been, the greatest surprise of all will be when he opens our eyes to see the great extent to which he was with us all along. The way to be prepared most fully for Christ's return is to be as close to him in his presence now as we can—and that includes his presence in the least of his little ones.

Bibliography

The following resources were used in the preparation of this commentary, especially the commentaries of Caird and Charles.

Arndt, William F., and F. Wilbur Gingrich. *A Greek-English Lexicon of the New Testament*. Trans. of Walter Bauer's *Griechisch-Deutsches Worterbuch*. . . . Fourth ed., rev., augmented. Chicago: The University of Chicago Press, 1952.

Ashcraft, Morris. "Revelation." In *The Broadman Bible Commentary*, vol. 12, ed. Clifton J. Allen. Nashville: Broadman Press, 1972.

Blevins, James L. *Revelation*. Knox Preaching Guides, ed. John H. Hayes. Atlanta: John Knox Press, 1984.

_____. *Revelation as Drama*. Nashville: Broadman Press, 1984.

Bromiley, Geoffrey W., ed. *The International Standard Bible Encyclopediea*, rev. Grand Rapids: William B. Eerdmans Publishing Co., 1986.

Buttrick, George A., ed. *The Interpreter's Dictionary of the Bible*. Nashville: Abingdon Press, 1962.

Caird, G. B. *The Revelation of St. John the Divine*. Harper's New Testament Commentaries, ed. Henry Chadwick. New York: Harper & Row Publishers, 1966.

Charles, R. H. *The Revelation of St. John*. The International Critical Commentary, eds. Driver, Pummer, and Briggs. Edinburgh: T. & T. Clark, 1920.

Charlesworth, James H. *The Old Testament Pseudepigrapha*. Garden City: Doubleday & Co., 1983.

Collins, Adela Yarbro. "The Apocalypse (Revelation)." In *The New Jerome Biblical Commentary*, eds. Brown, Fitzmeyer, and Murphey. Englewood Cliffs: Prentice Hall, 1990.

Darton, Michael, ed. *Modern Concordance to the New Testament*. Garden City: Doubleday & Co., Inc., 1976.

Friedrich, Gerhard, ed. *Theological Dictionary of the New Testament.* Trans. and ed. Geoffrey W. Bromiley. Grand Rapids: Wm. B. Eerdmans Publishing Co., 1974.

Kodell, Jerome. *The Catholic Bible Study Handbook.* Ann Arbor: Servant Books, 1985.

Perkins, Pheme. *Reading the New Testament: An Introduction.* New York: Paulist Press, 1978.

Schüssler Fiorenza, Elisabeth. *Invitation to the Book of Revelation.* Garden City: Image Books, 1981.

Schmithals, Walter. *The Apocalyptic Movement: Introduction and Interpretation.* Trans. John E. Steely. Nashville: Abingdon Press, 1975.

Appendix

A More Complete Explanation of the Meaning of the Number of the Beast in Revelation 13:28.

1. The text indicates in 13:17 that this is the number of the beast's name, and in 13:18 the Greek, literally translated, says: "The wisdom [or, key to understanding] is here: The one having intelligence, let him count the number of the beast: for it is the number of a man." Therefore, the number is not some non-specific, general symbol for someone; it is specifically the number of a particular individual.

2. We do not have the original Greek edition of Revelation; all we have are copies of copies. Most copies that we have say that the number is 666; however, a small but significant number say that the number is 616. Therefore, whatever explanation is used for 666 must also hold true for 616.

3. There was a Hebrew science called *gematria* which found significance in the fact that Hebrew letters were also used as numerals. A New Testament example of this may be seen in Matthew 1:17, where a listing of Jesus' family tree yields three sets of fourteen generations. The name "David" spelled in Hebrew is "DVD"; in the Hebrew alphabet a "D" is a 4 and a "V" is a 6: 4 + 6 + 4 = 14. Jesus is the son of David, a point very important to Matthew and his Hebrew Christian readers.

4. We have already said that both the head of the beast that did not die after being mortally wounded, as well as the first of the four horsemen, refer to Nero. Taking Nero's Greek name and transliterating it into Hebrew letters (it's a Hebrew number science, so one must transliterate the Greek letters into

Hebrew letters), NRON KSR (Neron Kaisar) = 666. If one uses the Latin form in Hebrew letters, one gets 616. Thus the name of Nero Caesar explains both numbers.